M000283492

songs of the isles

songs of the isles

Selections from *Carmina Gadelica*:
A new version with a commentary

Kathleen Jones

CANTERBURY
PRESS
Norwich

Copyright © Kathleen Jones 2004

First published in 2004 by the Canterbury Press Norwich
(a publishing imprint of Hymns Ancient & Modern Limited,
a registered charity)
St Mary's Works, St Mary's Plain,
Norwich, Norfolk, NR3 3BH

www.scm-canterburypress.co.uk

All rights reserved. No part of this publication may be reproduced,
stored in a retrieval system, or transmitted, in any form or by any means,
electronic, mechanical, photocopying or otherwise, without the
prior permission of the publisher, Canterbury Press

The Author has asserted her right under the
Copyright, Designs and Patents Act, 1988, to be
identified as the Author of this Work

British Library Cataloguing in Publication data

A catalogue record for this book is available
from the British Library

Maps by John Flower

ISBN 1-85311-584-3

Typeset in Minion and American Uncial
by Regent Typesetting, London
Printed and bound by
Biddles Ltd, www.biddles.co.uk

Contents

contents

Preface

The Isles of this study are the Hebrides, the islands which lie west of Scotland and north of Ireland. The Songs are better known as *Carmina Gadelica*, or Gaelic Songs, and some of them have been widely quoted in publications concerned with the 'golden age' of Celtic spirituality in the sixth to ninth centuries of the Christian era.

The Songs remained a purely oral tradition until the late nineteenth century, when Alexander Carmichael, a civil servant who worked in the Isles for many years, committed them to paper. He was called 'the Collector', not because he collected songs, but because he collected taxes: he was responsible for the assessment and collection of land taxes on the scattered crofts. As he travelled, he noted down the songs and hymns that he heard the Islanders crooning at their work. Sometimes the crooning was very soft, so that strangers should not overhear the words. There is a well-known incident in which one Islander implored Carmichael not to keep a record of his song, lest 'the cold eyes of foreign readers' should fall upon it. The paper was immediately destroyed.

Alexander Carmichael published two volumes of his work in a limited edition, 'sumptuously bound' at his own expense. He was much praised for his unique contribution to Scottish literature, and his obituary in *The Times* in 1912 described him as 'the most interesting personality in Gaelic Scotland'. Subsequently, three more volumes were published from his mass of papers; but in the current vogue for reductionist criticism, commentators have questioned both his sources and his methods. How could a late Victorian without academic training accurately record and translate Gaelic poems which he claims were composed so many centuries earlier? Do the Songs really represent Celtic beliefs and a way of life that has long since disappeared? Did he (consciously or subconsciously) select poems that fitted in with his own preconceptions of what this ancient Celtic society was like? Are the Songs anything more than a romantic exercise in nostalgia? Did he even write them himself?

Such questions need to be asked. I think they can be answered. Alexander Carmichael was no fiction writer. This sturdy, bearded Scot with his plain kilt and his staff was a scrupulously honest and painstaking reporter – so much so that his translations echo Gaelic speech patterns and grammatical constructions. Since they were published, academic research projects carried out by historians, geographers, archaeologists and other scholars have confirmed the picture he gives in his translations of how the Islanders lived and worked so many centuries earlier; and a careful reading of the Songs makes it clear that *he often did not realize the significance of what he recorded.* He notes, but does not understand, feasts and practices which in his own Presbyterian culture were dubbed 'Catholic' and sternly avoided; and as a patriotic Scot, he takes it for granted that the Songs are Scottish. They are not. Though the Isles have been under Scottish jurisdiction since the thirteenth century, the culture he describes is not Scottish in modern terms. In 'the age of the saints', Scotland was not yet a united nation. There were extensive Irish settlements, right across the Isles and on the mainland of what is now western Scotland. In fact, before they passed into Scottish jurisdiction in the thirteenth century, the Isles had been in the possession of Norway for two hundred years, and the Scots had to buy them from the king of Norway. Alexander Carmichael plainly did not know this. He writes of 'our dear Highland people', 'our beloved Highland people', but they were not Highlanders. He was setting down an ancient tradition that went far beyond his own range of historical knowledge.

The Songs give a vivid picture of the lives of the Islanders –

rejoicing at the birth of a child or a good harvest, glory at natural beauty, anguish in suffering, fear of attack from wild beasts or foreign invaders, fear of death. This is raw human experience in a harsh and often hazardous environment: they shout with joy, groan with pain, and sometimes yell in sheer terror. Alexander Carmichael could not possibly have invented all this. This quiet, decent Scotsman simply did not have the emotional range that would have taxed a Dickens or a Dostoevsky.

It is not possible to date the Songs with any accuracy. Nobody can say with certainty that they go back to 'the age of the saints' – Patrick and Brigid and Columba and the others whose names recur in their lines; but the teaching of the Celtic monks may have endured much longer in these remote islands, largely unaffected by war, conquest or religious upheaval, than in either Ireland or Scotland. What we can say is that the Songs reflect that teaching as it was understood by the Islanders and eventually set down by Alexander Carmichael. Their faith was firmly Trinitarian, untouched by the heresies and conflicts that swept across Europe. They understood that God was the Creator, the life-force who made and sustained the universe; that Jesus Christ died for sinful men and women; and that the Holy Spirit guided them and prodded their consciences. They had a devotion to the Virgin Mary and the saints that today attracts Catholics, and a knowledge of the Bible that attracts Protestants. They had a love of the natural world that fits well with our current preoccupation with eco-systems and the survival of our planet; and a sufficient undertow to a pre-Christian world of spells and incantations, omens and curses to guarantee the interest of antiquarians and New Age enthusiasts.

The Songs are, as Esther de Waal has noted in *The Celtic Way of Prayer*, 'a deep look at a deep past' (*The Celtic Way of Prayer*, 2003, p. ix). To date, they have been the preserve of writers on Celtic Christianity, many of them seeking a purer and apparently simpler faith than the one with which they have to contend in the twenty-first century, and of Gaelic orthographers, concerned to preserve the exact form of words of a disappearing language. Historians have not been much interested in the oral traditions of this small, non-literate culture; but an historical approach has something new to offer by dealing with a number of different contexts: the context in which the Songs evolved among the Islanders, probably over a thousand years ago, reflecting the teaching of the Celtic monks; the context of Alexander Carmichael, who got to know this oral tradition and translated the Songs in the later days of Queen Victoria; the context of his grandson, a professor of Celtic Studies, who inherited the Carmichael papers, and published further volumes before going off to join the Royal Navy in World War Two; and the contexts in which they have been analysed and criticized in more recent times.

Part 1 is an account of what is known about the world of the Islanders in the time of the Celtic saints, drawn from both early and modern sources. Part 2 is a new version of the Songs. Alexander Carmichael has been accused of 'archaizing' them to make them seem older than they are. This is surely a misunderstanding. What he has done is to set them down in the idiom of an elderly Gaelic-speaking Scot of his own day; but his habits of speech often get in the way of clear expression. Peasant farmers do not say things like, 'O Thou who broughtst me from the rest of last night', or 'Behold the Lightener of the stars'. Their speech is simpler and more direct. Carmichael also introduces Scottish terms that may puzzle non-Scottish readers. What is a 'foul foumart'? (Probably a stinking polecat.) How do you 'smoor' a fire? (A peat fire smoulders, and you bank it up for the night, to save having to 'borrow fire' from a neighbour in the morning.) Plain English helps. I have edited, re-arranged, paraphrased and added some explanatory notes. I hope that the result illustrates one important point: the poetry is in what the Islanders sang. It is still there when the obscuring features of the Victorian translations have been removed.

Part 3 is a study of the processes by which the Songs were collected, edited and eventually published, and the problems the editors encountered. Part 4 is an analysis of the criticisms that have been made of their work, and the controversies that have ensued.

My aim has been to make the Songs accessible to a wider English-speaking public; to make them more comprehensible by describing the contexts in which they have been developed, translated and analysed; and to lead some readers back to *Carmina Gadelica* in the original form with a greater understanding of the source-material. Perhaps the Islanders, now linked to the outside world by the aeroplane and the Internet, will no longer mind foreign eyes falling on their heritage. I hope that the 'foreigners' of the wider Church can draw strength from it.

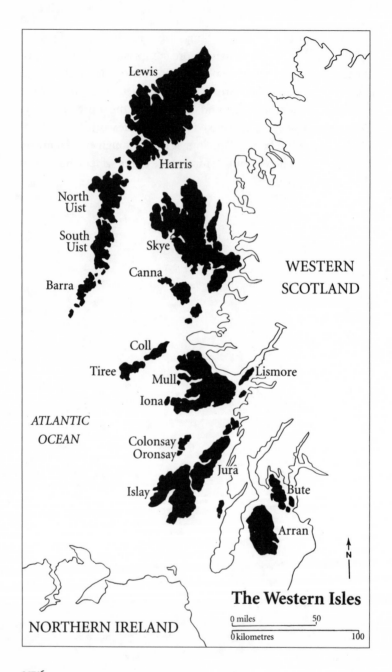

Lewis

Harris

North
Uist

South
Uist

Barra

Skye

Canna

WESTERN
SCOTLAND

Coll

Tiree

Mull

Iona

Lismore

ATLANTIC
OCEAN

Colonsay
Oronsay

Jura

Islay

Bute

Arran

N

The Western Isles

0 miles   50

0 kilometres   100

NORTHERN IRELAND

ATLANTIC OCEAN

SCANDINAVIA

N

EUROPE

Cadiz

Rome

Constantinople

Athens

NORTH AFRICA

Western Sea Routes

0 miles 500

0 kilometres 1000

Jerusalem

Alexandria

Part 1

the world
of the islanders

the world of the islanders

There are said to be over 500 islands in the Hebrides. The larger ones are as much as 40 or 50 miles in length, while others are tiny rocky outcrops. The Outer Hebrides – Lewis, Harris, North Uist, Benbecula, South Uist, Eriskay and Barra, working from north to south – form an arc, once a mountain chain, over 100 miles long on the edge of the Atlantic. The Inner Hebrides, more sheltered, include the large islands of Mull and Skye, and smaller islands like Arran, Lismore and Bute, which are all but surrounded by the Scottish mainland. Nowhere in the Isles is more than 50 miles from the mainland of either Scotland or Ireland, and nearly all the inhabitants live within sight and sound of the sea.

The total population of the Isles today is in the region of 27,000. There are a few harbour towns where the ferries dock and the tourists come in the summer, but inland there is nothing corresponding to the English or Scottish village. Most people live on crofts dotted about the landscape in valleys between the great granite rocks. The winters are long, and in December there may be no more than five or six hours of daylight. The climate, so pleasant in the long warm days and light nights of summer, is often harsh in winter. Islanders can be cut off from the outside world for days or weeks at a time by high winds and stormy seas.

Though the Isles have a distinctive culture of their own, they are not all alike. The flat plains and moors of Harris and Lewis

3

are very different from the mountains of Jura, or the black and forbidding Cuillins of Skye. Tiree has no trees, but the soil is fertile, and in Celtic times it was the 'granary' from which other islands imported the cereal crops they could not grow on their own thin soil. Colonsay was where the stone of the distinctive Celtic crosses, still to be found on most of the isles, was quarried. Bute, sheltered in the Firth of Clyde, is known for its exotic plants. On some of the larger islands there are lochs, pine forests and waterfalls, and red deer can sometimes be seen posing against the skyline; but the sea is always close. Dolphins leap in the water, seals lumber out of the sounds to lie on the rocks; and overhead, eagles and many kinds of seabirds wheel in the sky.

The sea routes

Today the Isles are remote areas of great natural beauty, but in the sixth to the ninth centuries they were not remote from outside influence: they were situated on one of the main sea highways of Europe. The men of the Isles were all sailors – they had to be, because their communications were essentially maritime. The seas round their shores were alive with boats, large and small. An understanding of the importance of the sea routes in the 'age of the saints', mapped out in detail by Professor Emrys Bowen of University College, Cardiff,[1] has revolutionized thinking about patterns of communication to the Celtic lands. His *Saints, Seaways and Settlements in the Celtic Lands* (1969) summarized and amplified a number of earlier archaeological and geohistorical studies, and led to a new interest in the Eastern Mediterranean influences on the Celtic lands. Professor Barry Cunliffe's *Facing the Ocean* (2000) gives a vivid picture of a world in which sea travel reached from the shores of Asia Minor and north Africa to the lands on the rim of the Atlantic, and trading vessels made regular runs of surprising length.[2]

The harbours of Gibraltar and Cadiz were the gateways to the world beyond the Mediterranean. The Romans called the Mediterranean *Mare Nostrum* – Our Sea – but by the sixth century Rome had fallen to the Ostrogoths, and the remnants of the Roman Empire were being ruled from Constantinople. In north Africa, the Vandals had swept into former Roman cities, but the great sea routes to Alexandria, Constantinople and Antioch were still open. From Gibraltar and Cadiz, the traders came north, using the harbours and rivers of the Iberian peninsula and France, sometimes carrying their goods overland across Brittany and Cornwall to avoid the dangerous currents round Finistère and the Lizard, and then on to such harbours as Cork and Wexford and the Solway Firth. The mother of St Ninian, Scotland's earliest saint (*c*.362–432), is said to have been a Spanish princess – probably the daughter of a chief. At Whithorn, where Ninian built his monastery, excavations have revealed evidence of a trading centre.[3]

Sailing south from Scandinavia via the Orkneys came the Vikings in their big cargo boats, known as *knorr*. They traded as far afield as Greenland and Kiev in Russia. Sometimes they came as pirates, but there was little in the way of booty to be found in the Isles. Usually they came as traders, until the late eighth century, sometimes settling peacefully. The Norwegians are credited with the invention of oilskins to protect seafarers against the wet and the biting winds: fleeces smeared with cod liver oil.[4]

The seagoing vessels from the Mediterranean brought supplies such as salt and wine and pottery, trading their goods for meat, fresh water and hides. Irish leather and Irish shoes were famous. The Islanders probably only encountered the big ships when they sailed to the major ports on the coasts of Scotland or Ireland. Their own boats were coracles or curraghs – timber frames covered with hide. They had a very shallow draught, and so could ride the waves like a seagull instead of having to plough through them. They were not only tiny fishing boats: some could take up to 40 rowers, and some had sails and quite complicated tackle.[5] They were frequently used to transport cattle and sheep from one island to another. The larger curraghs were capable of travelling as far south as Cornwall in good weather. The routes to western Scotland and southern

Ireland, and from one island to another, would have been well known to the Islanders. Caledonian MacBrayne ferries, which ply many of them today, have a very long history of seamanship behind them. The sailors navigated by the stars, and feared fog and sea-frets, which might blind them and drive them on to the rocks.

The home life of the Islanders

The people of the Isles were crofters, and they lived liminally – between land and sea, between earth and sky. Each man had his own holding for himself and his family. On the larger islands there were chiefs of some standing who could summon the men to defend their property in case of outside attack; but for the most part, the crofters lived lives of sturdy and sometimes precarious independence. They were patriarchal, as peasant societies usually are, because the men had to do the heavy work and the women were often pregnant. The men farmed, fished, hunted and fought when necessary. The women milked the cows, fed the hens, spun and wove the cloth, made the clothes, bore the children, cooked, tended the sick and laid out the dead. Their houses were usually circular, made of whatever material was available: timber or dry stone if it was found locally, and reeds and mud if that was all they had. Each house would have had a barn or grain-pit, and enclosures for livestock.[6]

It was not a simple life. Subsistence farming is very complicated, and requires a variety of different skills. It was a life of unremitting hard work just to survive. In times of plenty, most crofting families would have eaten well – game from the woods, fish from the sea and the rivers, eggs from the hens, meat when a chicken or a sheep or cow was killed. A family that owned a cow would have milk and butter. Grain was a staple – wheat, oats or barley, depending on the soil – but when the grain supply became low, and the hay ran out, famine was not far away for families and their farm animals alike. Good weather meant the difference between sufficiency and starvation. If the crops were still thin and green in August, there were months of lean living ahead. A bitter winter meant an anxious time looking for the first green shoots in the spring, and rescuing the newborn lambs and keeping them warm by the fire. There were of course no potatoes, but they grew other root vegetables and herbs, and had fruits and nuts in season if the soil would support them. Without sugar, they were dependent for sweetness on honey – either from the bees or stored in flowers such as clover and heather. They made spruce beer and mead for their feasts. The climate is thought to have been warmer than it is now, but it is not likely that vineyards flourished on these windswept coasts. Wine would have had to come from the traders. Wealth was reckoned in cattle and sheep: there was no metal currency, and exchange was effected by barter, although coins from the Mediterranean countries have been found in the trading settlements, which must have had something of an international character.[7]

Pre-Christian beliefs

The festivals the Islanders kept may have been Druidic in origin, but we know little about Druidic worship. The Druids had no temples, worshipping in groves and by rivers, so there are no buildings to be excavated. Though they were apparently literate, they were a priestly caste who passed on their knowledge by oral transmission, so they kept no records. Possibly Druidism reached the larger Isles, where there are standing stones to testify to some sort of organized worship; the standing stones of Callanish on Lewis are reckoned to rank next to Stonehenge in importance. However, Richard Sharpe points out in his commentary on *Adamnan's Life of Columba* that *drui* was the Old Irish word for a pagan priest, and the plural was *druid*.[8] It was not until the eighteenth century that a connection was suggested with Druidic cults in England.[9]

The Islanders, like most farmers, were probably prepared to propitiate any gods who would guarantee them a good harvest. They practised a nature religion in which the feasts were essentially connected with the yearly cycle of plant and animal life. Imbolc, in

February or early March, was the planting time, and the time when ewes began to lactate in anticipation of lambing. In Gaelic it was called *Ceud Mhios an Earraich,* the first month of spring. Beltane, in May, was the growing time. Lammas or Lughnasad, in August, was the time to begin the harvest, and Samhainn in late autumn was the time of clearing up and settling in for the winter.

Ceremonial fires were of much significance in a damp and rainy climate where the only means of making new fire was to rub two hard pieces of wood (preferably oak) together, and the fire ceremonies of Beltane and Samhainn seem well established. There were religious ceremonies for seed-time and harvest, and at the summer and winter solstices.

The Islanders' cosmology must have been fairly limited. They knew the operations of the sun, the moon and the stars, because they were heavily dependent on natural light. They would have known the stars from the planets, as the ancient Greek and Roman world did, and clear, unpolluted skies must have made star-gazing a pleasure. If Barry Cunliffe's thesis in *Facing the Ocean* is right, they would have heard of only three continents, Europe, Asia and Africa, grouped round the Mediterranean Sea. Beyond those land masses was The Ocean, a place of fabled monsters and dark nightmares.[10] It is unlikely that they knew that the world is round. Alexander Carmichael translates the Gaelic word *cruinne* as 'the globe', which is its modern meaning; but it is related to the Latin *corona,* and in pre-Copernican times it may only have meant the stars in their courses, the whole marvellous panoply of the heavens.

Folk beliefs older than Druidism, involving banshees, rock sprites, water nymphs, giants and fairies, were never entirely banished from the crofters' minds. Many of these invisible inhabitants of the Celtic Otherworld were thought to be malevolent, and they merged with the visible enemies – the bears and wolves and boars, the steep cliffs and the dangerous currents – to create a sense of insecurity. Life on the crofts was very dangerous. Many of the later Christian prayers are fervent pleas for protection which must have had pre-Christian origins.

The coming of Christianity

We know that there were Christians in Ireland well before the year 431, when Pope Celestine I sent his envoy Palladius to investigate their beliefs and regulate their worship. (This is one of the few dates that we can take as reliable, since it is in the Vatican records.) The pope addressed his mission *ad Scottos in Christum credentes*: 'to the Scots believing in Christ',[11] so they were known not all to be pagans. Ireland was then known to the distant papacy as *Scotia maior*, and what is now Scotland as *Scotia minor*. Palladius landed near Arklow or Wicklow, and his commission was to regularize existing Christian institutions and root out heresy, not to engage in a new mission. No doubt earlier priests had come with the traders from France and Spain, and some may have stayed to minister to local congregations.

'Scots' from Ulster had migrated from *Scotia maior* and settled in *Scotia minor*, where they formed a large colony known as *Dál Riata* or Dalriada, after the kingdom of the same name in the Antrim area.[12] In this period there was no clear distinction between Ireland and Scotland, least of all in the islands which linked the two. In both, tribal chiefs were gradually consolidating their lands and becoming local kings, making war on one another or forging local alliances as circumstances dictated. The Highlands of what is now Scotland were held by the Picts; the Lowlands, apart from Dalriada, were areas of conflict between the Brythons from Wales in the west and the Northumbrians in the east.[13] The first claim to be king of a united Scotland did not come until 843, when Kenneth II Macalpin, a Scot who had succeeded his father two years earlier, made peace with the Picts.[14]

Nearly three centuries before that, in or about 561, St Columba left Ireland, landed on Iona and began his mission to the Isles, bringing his Irish religious heritage with him. Christianity had developed in Ireland in a form very different from the Roman system based on bishops and dioceses. The reasons for this were purely practical: the terrain was simply inappropriate. Lacking cities for bishops' seats, and a road system to enable them to exercise jurisdiction over their dioceses, Christian institutions in Ireland were based on monasteries, a system learned from the Desert Fathers of Egypt and the Middle East.

At the time Columba sailed for Iona, the Western Roman Empire had crumbled under the attacks of barbarian tribes. Justinian, the emperor, ruled from Constantinople, and the remaining imperial territories in Italy were governed by an exarch based in Ravenna. The Byzantine influence can still be seen in the celebrated mosaics of Ravenna, including those in the great basilica of San Vitale. Rome, which had been repeatedly sacked, was not the religious centre. Though Justinian's general Belisarius[15] was trying to stem the advances of the Ostrogoths in Italy, the Visigoths in Spain and the Vandals in north Africa, many wealthy Romans had abandoned their estates and withdrawn to the Holy Land, which was the main pilgrimage centre. The civilization they had taken for granted was breaking up.[16]

The monastic system that the Irish Christians adopted had developed in the Thebaïd of Upper Egypt in the third and fourth centuries, when Christians in the Middle East had fled from persecution by the Roman emperors. Though the most celebrated of the Desert Fathers is the anchorite St Antony,[17] the model that was more widely used was that of Pachomius, a former officer in the Roman army who first set up a communal monastery at Tabbenesi on the Upper Nile about the year 318.[18] In these monasteries, Roman military organization and Christian asceticism combined in a way of life that attracted many followers, both men and women. St Jerome (341–410), one of the great Fathers of the Church,[19] became a monk in the Syrian desert for five years, and later visited the Thebaïd before settling in Bethlehem to work on his translation of the Bible, which ultimately became the basis of the Vulgate. His wealthy patroness and colleague St Paula founded two monasteries in Jerusalem, one for men and one for women.[20] By Columba's time, the hills around Jerusalem were crowded with monastic foundations – communal monasteries, *lavras* or lauras, like Mar Saba where the monks lived separately, meeting only for worship or occasional meals, and anchorite cells. Jerusalem was the religious centre of the world.

In the fourth century, the monastic system spread to Asia Minor, where Basil, Bishop of Caesarea[21] and his brothers Peter of Sebaste and Gregory of Nyssa established monasteries, and their sister Macrina developed a religious house for women in their family home at Pontus.[22] A century or so later it reached Rome, where St Benedict became known as 'the father of Western monasticism', following the foundation of his monasteries at Monte Cassino and Subiaco;[23] but despite the great influence of the Benedictine movement on the continent of Europe, it developed in the former Roman territories as an adjunct to the diocesan system, under the control of bishops, not as a replacement for it.

Ireland was more like the Upper Thebaïd, or Syria or war-torn Palestine, where there was no effective diocesan organization and each monastery, under its abbot, was virtually independent, though they formed 'families' with allegiance to common founders. During the fifth and early sixth centuries, a wave of monastic foundations had become the basis of Christian learning and Christian mission. The names of the great monastic founders – Ailbe of Enda, Ciaran of Clonmacnoise, Ciaran of Saighir and others – are part of Irish history.[24] They all introduced Eastern-style monasticism, which must have reached them by the sea routes. It was ascetic and strongly penitential – a fact which should give the lie to the charge that the Irish monasteries were affected by the Pelagian heresy.[25]

The Irish Penitentials describe a very firm discipline based on the concept of original sin.[26] The daily recital of the Offices, hard physical labour, hours of studying Latin texts, long fasts and penitential exercises made no concessions to the flesh. The head of the monastery was the abbot, and the bishop was a missioner subject to his authority. Bishops visited the courts of local kings, evangelizing and counselling the laity. They had ritual functions – Baptism, Confirmation and Ordination – and were essentially outreach workers.[27] Monasteries were centres of prayer and learning that built up their own traditions, often on a basis of common clan membership. Copies of manuscripts reached them by the sea routes – there were many translations of Greek and Hebrew texts coming from the Middle East. They were written on vellum (calf skin), usually with a quill from a swan or a goose, or a sharp-pointed reed. Some of the manuscripts which came from Alexandria were badly copied and poorly translated. Copies of Jerome's manuscripts, rigorous and exact, and translated not only in the Holy Land but in a cell adjacent to the place of Christ's Nativity, were eagerly sought, passed from monastery to monastery and recopied. When St Finnian of Moville in County Down travelled to the Continent in the mid-sixth century and came back with a new copy of part of St Jerome's work, all the people went down to the harbour to welcome him on his return and rejoice in this precious possession.[28]

The faith that Columba and his monks took to the Isles gave the Islanders a very good grasp of the doctrine of the Trinity as expressed in the Creeds. Christ the Redeemer existed before all time, one with God the Creator and the ever-present Holy Spirit. The power that created and upheld their known world and the power that saved sinful men were one and the same. The Virgin Mary, greatly respected as the human mother of Christ, was an object of much prayer and many requests for protection, being the chief of the saints. Angels and archangels carried out God's work on earth – and some of the manuscripts circulating in Columba's time may have come from Jewish apocryphal literature rather than from the texts that eventually constituted the Bible. The names of some angels invoked by the Islanders are not found in the Old and New Testaments, or even the biblical Apocrypha. The chief archangel was St Michael, the warrior, who protected the weak, supported a righteous cause in battle, and took the soul at the point of death to Christ for judgement and mercy. The 12 Apostles were reverenced, and assumed, as in many medieval paintings, to have included St Paul rather than Matthias, who replaced Judas Iscariot (Acts 1.23–5). The Islanders frequently invoked the saints who had gone before and who would pray for them in heaven. It is important to note that ancient Celtic literature uses the word 'saint' in the sense in which St Paul uses it, when he writes 'to all God's beloved in Rome, who are called to be saints' (Rom. 1.7) or 'to the church that is in Corinth, to those who are sanctified in Christ Jesus, called to be saints' (I Cor. 1.2). The centralized Roman Catholic procedures for beatification and sanctification which attracted much superstition are of a considerably later date.[29]

Two Irish saints, St Patrick and St Brigid, came to have a special place in the Islanders' prayers. Patrick, whose dates are usually given as 390–461, came from somewhere on the west coast of northern England or southern Scotland.[30] He was captured as a boy by Irish raiders, and spent six years in Ireland as a slave, before returning there in later life as a missioner. He used the shamrock, the three-in-one plant that grew freely in the countryside, as a symbol of the Trinity. His pupils and successors established monasteries which became centres of learning. There is evidence that Patrick knew part of St Jerome's translation of the Scriptures: he quotes from it in his *Confession*. Patrick tells his own story in the *Confession* and the *Letter to Coroticus*, both of which are generally accepted as authentic. Somehow these two documents survived the devastation and ruin of the following centuries and contributed to Patrick's adoption as Ireland's patron saint. They must have been well known in Columba's day, particularly in his native Ulster, where Patrick commenced his mission.

The historical St Brigid (Bridget, Bride, Brigida) has a more complicated background.[31] The dates usually assigned to her are 461–524, which suggests that she may still have been alive when Columba was born in 521. To him and his monks, she would not have been the half-legendary figure excessive piety later made her, but a real person who had been known by many during her lifetime. Brigid was the daughter of a chief and one of his bondmaids. After attempting to force her into an advantageous marriage, her father set her free and allowed her to enter the religious life. She was taught by the aged Bishop Mel, one of Patrick's disciples, and founded a women's community in Kildare. Strong and persistent traditions say that she was well loved by local people, good at settling feuds and helping women to bear their children, and particularly renowned for helping cows to calve and give milk. Through a coincidence of names, her reputation became linked to that of a pre-Christian, possibly Druidic, goddess named Brigg, and after Columba's time with a Scandinavian goddess named Brigantia. As the principal woman saint of Ireland, she was often compared to the Virgin Mary, and sometimes called 'the Mary of the Gael'. There was even a legend, based on her skill as a midwife, that she was the innkeeper's wife who had reputedly helped the Virgin Mary to bear the Christ-child.

Columba and the monks of Iona

Columba, who was to become the apostle of Celtic Christianity in the Isles and later in Scotland, landed on Iona about the year 563. He was a man of position and consequence – a member of the powerful southern Uí Neill of Ulster, and already an abbot, the founder of three monasteries, at Derry, Kells and Durrow. He was a scholar, and much concerned with the acquisition and copying of Gospel manuscripts. According to his biographer, Adamnan, he went to stay on one occasion at the monastery of St Finnian of Clonard, and surreptitiously copied a precious manuscript. Finnian found out, and demanded the copy. King Diarmid of the northern Uí Neill ruled that Columba must hand it over. Relations between the northern Uí Neill and Columba's branch of the clan deteriorated, and there was a battle at Cuill-Drebne. Columba blessed his own side before the battle, and when they were defeated, he was sent into exile.[32]

With him to the island known as Hy or Iona went 12 of his monks, all members of his own clan. The island is only about three miles long and less than a mile wide – two clumps of rock with a dry valley between. There are no lakes or rivers, so there would have been no source of fresh water apart from rain. A few stunted trees, bent by the wind, would have given no hope of timber for building; and the thin grass was only good enough for sheep – it would not support cows, like the lush green pastures he had left in Ulster. Columba must have stood with his back to his beloved Ireland, looking towards the mountains of Mull, and realized that this really was exile of the most stringent kind. Fortunately, his kinsmen and monks from his Irish monasteries supported the new venture for a time, taking goods and supplies across to Iona until the exiles were able to fend for themselves. In later years Columba was able to return to Ireland on a number of occasions to attend synods or conferences, and he kept some links with the monasteries he had founded there; but one Irish story illustrates the harshness of the conditions in which he and his companions lived.

They acquired one cow, presumably brought from Ireland, which must have meant a tricky journey in a coracle. The monks were thankful for the milk and butter; but Columba observed that a poor old crofting woman living near the monastry had no cow, and her staple diet was nettle soup. There was no shortage of nettles. He decided that if poor crofters could survive on nettle soup, so could he; but the monk who did the cooking was afraid that his abbot would become ill on such a restricted diet, so he surreptitiously introduced milk into the soup through a hollow reed. Columba continued to flourish, and the other monks in the community decided that they too could live on nettle soup. The cow did not produce enough milk to provide fortified soup all round, so the cook had to confess his stratagem. Columba was at first angry, then he gave a great shout of laughter, and decided that they should all eat more reasonably in future.

Iona must have seemed a very small place to a man of such talents and energies. The island became the centre of a mission to the Isles, then later to the Picts of *Scotia minor*, when Columba and a group of monks including Comgall, the founder of the great Irish missionary college of Benn Chorr or Bangor, travelled up the lochs all the way to the head of Loch Ness. The Pictish King Brude, secure in his castle with his wizards and warlocks, ordered the gates to be bolted against the invaders. Columba, who was a big man with a carrying voice, raised one huge arm, and chanted Psalm 44: 'By thy help we will throw back our enemies; in thy name will we trample down our adversaries.' The gates were hastily unbolted, and the party went in to convert Brude, wizards, warlocks and all.[33] Modern writers think that this expedition may have been in part a diplomatic one.[34] By that time Columba was on better terms with the king at Tara, and one of the results was to secure the position of the Irish settlers in *Dál Riata* against attack by the Picts.

Through the monks, the learning of the Irish monasteries was transmitted to the Islanders and their families. The monks read and worshipped in Latin, but they spoke the vernacular Goidelic or Gaelic, and it was in this language that the people of the Isles memorized what they were taught, and turned it into poetry of their own. Poetry is a powerful mnemonic. Rhyme, metre, alliteration and repetition all help in recalling the words.

The Irish monks went to many of the Isles – some to set up monasteries on the larger islands like Mull or Harris or Lewis, some to become virtually parish priests to smaller communities, some to live as hermits on tiny islands. They had their own regular runs by coracle from island to island. The Islanders loved Columba, who was much admired for his physical strength in pulling a coracle up on the beach, and his loud voice, which could be heard above the crashing of the waves. He was a humble man, and like Brigid, he acquired the reputation of being a very helpful saint. He could be relied on to cure a sick cow or bring a coracle safely home. Other saints of the Irish tradition might be appealed to for particular purposes, but Columba was an all-round saint, and for many Islanders a personal friend, because he had lived among them. His name became woven into their prayers – 'kind Columba', 'beloved Colum'.

The Islanders appear to have been well versed in the Bible, though they would have been unable to read the Latin manuscripts that were the only sources available at the time. In the larger centres the monks may have run small schools, but these would have been largely for future monks, and possibly for the sons of noblemen. The laymen and laywomen of the Isles must have listened carefully to the monks' teaching. If they sometimes confused St James the Great with St James the Less, or thought that St Paul was a fisherman like St Peter (the two share the same feast day) this is understandable in the circumstances. They learned the Psalms and the canticles, and reflected them in their own poems. A common practice among the Celtic monks was to recite all 150 Psalms aloud every day – preferably while standing in the cold water of the sea or a river to subdue the flesh. By the time they reached the end of Psalm 150, 'Let everything that has breath, praise the Lord', they must have been fairly breathless themselves. There are stories in the Lives of the saints of young novices taking a shovel of burning coals from the monastery to make a fire on the shore or the bank to warm a monk when he emerged from this exhausting exercise. If their aprons were not singed, this was accounted a miracle; but of course the aprons were made of leather, and would not have singed easily if the boy holding the shovel was careful.

Beyond the orthodox Christianity of the monks, the Islanders retained many older beliefs. The Celtic monks were tolerant, building on existing beliefs and giving them a Christian significance rather than suppressing them. This was also the policy of the Roman Church at this time. Pope Gregory the Great sent instructions to St Augustine of Canterbury early in his English mission to tell him to build his churches on the sites of pagan temples, and use pagan feast days as the dates for Christian holy days, so that the people might 'more readily come to desire the joys of the spirit'.[35] Stories of dramatic confrontations with 'pagan' forces, like Murchiu's account of St Patrick's challenge to the High King at Tara,[36] are probably the inventions of later and less tolerant chroniclers. Patrick is said to have lit a great Paschal fire at Easter to oppose the king's right to give 'new fire' to his people at Beltane, and to have followed it with miracles; but Beltane fell in May, too late for Easter, and the Christian ceremony of the Paschal fire did not develop until the ninth century. Patrick himself does not mention such an incident, which would have been a key stage in his mission; and he never claimed to work miracles.

The existing feasts of the Islanders were easily fitted into the cycle of the Christian year, with a new symbolism for fire as representing the triumph of light over darkness. Imbolc, the planting time, became St Brigid's feast day, 1 February; Beltane was replaced by the movable feast of Easter; the summer solstice became St John the Baptist's feast day, 24 June; Lammas or Lugnasadh became All Hallows or All Saints Day, 1 November (hence 'Hallowe'en' on the previous night); and Christmas replaced the winter solstice, celebrating the Incarnation.[37]

The Islanders would have had no difficulty with the doctrine of the Trinity, because their existing religious tradition was essentially triadic. Gods, goddesses and wizards commonly came in threes. They prayed to the Trinity, the Virgin, the angels and the saints to guard their families, prosper their crops, lead their sheep and cattle to good pasturing, keep them safe when they hunted in the woods, and preserve their little boats from the hazards of the sea. So ancient folklore became interwoven with Christian teaching, to become a working faith for practical people. The old religion was not exclusive or dogmatic, but essentially eclectic, making adaptation easy. Scholars have long tried to discover the names of Celtic gods, but apart from Lugg (hence Lugnasadh or Lammas) and Brigg (who became Brigid), there seems to have been no generalized use.[38] The gods were often local ones, with local names and local functions. They were not to be worshipped, but merely propitiated or besought. The teaching of the Celtic monks, with its tremendous doctrines of the Creation, the Fall, the redemption of the world through Jesus Christ and the coming of the Holy Spirit, did not conflict with earlier beliefs. It fitted over them, giving them a new significance and a new direction.

A changing world

Other missions made bases on Iona for a time – Comgall had an out-station there for the missionary monks of Benn Chorr.[39] The tiny island must have been fairly swarming with monks; but Columba's foundation was the one that became established and grew in influence. Missions went to the Picts, and to the people of the mainland Dalriada; but while this work was being consolidated, and parallel developments were being made by the Celtic Christians in Wales, Cornwall and Brittany, the Roman Church sent its own mission under St Augustine to Britain in 597, the year of Columba's death. Pope Gregory the Great planned to divide the English kingdoms into 12 dioceses, with an archbishop in London and an archbishop in York.

Bede of Jarrow records in considerable detail how circumstances forced the modification of these plans: how the Celtic monks under their abbot Aidan went to Northumbria, making their base not at York but at Lindisfarne, and developed missions in Mercia, East Anglia and southern Scotland, while the missionaries from Rome worked from Canterbury, setting up dioceses in the south of England. Conflict was inevitable, and in 664/5 the two sides finally came to confrontation at the Synod of Whitby.[40]

To Roman eyes, the Celtic monks must have looked distinctly un-Roman, and therefore uncivilized. Instead of a neat tonsure, they wore their hair shaved at the front and long and straggly at the back. Instead of well-made habits of smooth cloth, they wore rough homespun habits. Though they read Latin easily enough, and their services were conducted in Latin, they probably spoke it rather hesitantly, and they had an unsettling way of translating prayers and hymns into the vernacular for their congregations. The monastery at Whitby, ruled by the redoubtable St Hilda, had even encouraged a former cowherd named Caedmon to become a monk, and compose long religious poems in the Northumbrian dialect.[41] Celtic churches were simply huts, devoid of the stone architecture, religious paintings and jewelled crucifixes that

Roman monks found aids to worship. Celtic clergy did not wear elaborate vestments and their services were said or chanted in a harsh manner, without the smooth musicality of Gregorian chant. The services, with all those Psalms and the seemingly endless recital of the names of outlandish saints whom the Romans had never heard of, must have seemed interminable. In short, the whole enterprise lacked *dignitas*, and the Romans clearly suspected that it was heretical as well.

At the Synod of Whitby in 664/5, the matter of the date of Easter, on which all the differences between the two sides seemed to hang, was resolved in favour of the Roman party.[42] Bede, who was born in 673 and sent to the monastic school at the age of seven, must have been taught by monks who had been at the Synod, and knew both sides of the debate. In came the diocesan bishops and the diocesan officials, the paintings and the jewelled crucifixes, the relics and Gregorian chant. The Irish monks were withdrawn to Iona, and Northumbrians like St Cuthbert were left to make the best of some painful changes.[43]

The Islanders would probably have known little about these issues in Britain. Even when the Iona community followed the Irish Church in 716 by making a formal submission to Rome, the transition to Roman jurisdiction and the Roman style of worship was very slow. Kenneth II Macalpin, first king of a united Scotland, had Celtic monks at his court in Dunoon in the 840s.[44] The Roman Church concentrated on the power centres of mainland Britain and was not much concerned with the Celtic fringe. It was only when the Celtic monks had developed missions in mainland Britain with remarkable success that alarm bells rang in Rome.

The most potent threat to the church in the Isles was to come in the ninth century from another quarter – not from Rome but Scandinavia. There had always been risks from Norwegian pirates: in 618 a monastery on the island of Eigg, near Skye, had been attacked during the First Mass of Easter, and the monks burned alive with Donan, their abbot. A woman living on Eigg had a land dispute with the monks, and is said to have told the pirates when the monks would be least prepared and most vulnerable. The story is told in several Irish chronicles.[45]

The Norwegians, with little habitable land of their own, had begun to colonize the Shetlands, the Orkneys, the Hebrides, Sutherland and Caithness, but usually without much bloodshed. In the ninth century attacks, chiefly by the Danes, were much fiercer, and the sight of the *dreki*, or warships, approaching was a matter of dread. The light Celtic curraghs and coracles were no match for these formidable war machines.[46] The monasteries, by that time more prosperous, made tempting targets. In 825 an Irish monk named Dicuil wrote that monks had gone to live as far north as Iceland and the Faroes. They had been established there for 'roughly a hundred years' before the attacks drove them out. In the end, 'those who could escape went hurriedly, leaving their Gospel books, their crucifixes, and even their pastoral staffs behind'. There were no longer monks praising God in these distant places – only sheep, and 'a great many kinds of sea fowl'.[47] The monastery on Iona was repeatedly attacked. In 825 it was set on fire and many of the monks were massacred. The remaining monks finally withdrew to the safety of Kells in Ireland, taking Columba's relics with them.[48]

The Isles were technically Norwegian territory for about two centuries, though it would probably be inaccurate to say that Norway 'ruled' them, because there would have been little to rule once the sea traffic declined and the trading centres no longer operated; but there are still Norse place names in the Outer Hebrides, and Norse was spoken on Lewis until the fifteenth century.[49] But once Scotland was united in the ninth century, Scottish kings began to take an interest in these neighbouring territories, if only to avoid having a potential enemy so close at hand. In the second half of the eleventh century the Scottish king Malcolm Canmore[50] visited Iona with his queen, who was to become St Margaret of Scotland.

Margaret was a Saxon princess, educated by Benedictines at the court of Edward the Confessor. Over four centuries had elapsed since Columba went to King Brude's castle, and two and a half since the Celtic monks in Scotland had officially submitted to Roman jurisdiction. She found dissident Celtic monks in remote parts of Scotland, many of them hermits in the wilder places, in a sorry state. They were called 'Culdees', a corruption of the Irish *Ceili Dé*, a monastic reform movement of the eighth century; but lacking continued contact with Iona or the Irish monasteries, the movement had sadly deteriorated. Turgot, Queen Margaret's Benedictine confessor and later her biographer, found the Culdees 'barbarous'.[51] They were mostly unlettered, and their rites had deteriorated (at least in his estimation) into mumbo-jumbo. They did not receive Holy Communion, saying that they were sinful men, and unworthy. Some of them did not keep Lenten fasts or even Easter. They stood in church instead of kneeling, and they kept the Jewish Sabbath, on Saturday, and worked on Sundays.

Turgot is a prejudiced witness, and the contempt he felt for the last few Celtic Christians in Scotland comes through in his account. Queen Margaret, her Saxon words interpreted in Gaelic by her terrifying husband, managed to persuade many to follow Benedictine use; but some retreated to the more remote areas of the Highlands, and continued to follow their traditional customs.

Margaret and Malcolm made a pilgrimage to Iona in 1072, restoring and endowing the monastery, and putting it in the hands of the Benedictines; but the Hebrides were still officially Norwegian. The Norwegians had accepted Christianity, and in 1164 Iona was included in the diocese of Man and the Isles, under the jurisdiction of the archbishop of Trondheim. The Isles were not finally ceded to Scotland until 1266, when Haakon IV of Norway sold his title under the terms of the Treaty of Perth.[52]

A proud Scottish nation needed a patron saint; but the Irish Columba and the half-Spanish Ninian were not suitable role models. In time, Queen Margaret would be accorded sainthood in the Roman Calendar, but she was a Saxon. If the Scots could not find a Scottish patron, they needed a saint of unimpeachable qualifications, and they found one in St Andrew, brother of Simon Peter. The story of how St Andrew became the patron saint of Scotland (he is also one of the patron saints of Russia) strains credulity.[53] A monk in Patras, the Greek city where St Andrew was reputedly executed, is said to have had a vision in which he was told to take the saint's relics 'to the ends of the earth'. He was miraculously transported to the place now known as St Andrews on the east coast of Fifeshire, where he converted the local chief, whose name was Angus or Hungus. The saltire, or diagonal cross of St Andrew, was not known in Scotland until the tenth century, and it seems likely that if any relics were actually taken to Scotland, they were taken there by some early pilgrim or knight during the Crusades. However, Andrew clearly outranked Columba, whose association with the Culdees must have been as uncomfortable as his Irish origins. Ian Bradley describes how 'the triumph of Andrew over Columba' represented 'a steady shift eastwards in the centre of ecclesiastical and political gravity in mediaeval Scotland'; but Columba 'remained an infinitely more popular figure among the Scottish people', particularly in the country districts.[54]

The Reformation

In the Isles, these changes in the great world beyond their waters probably had little effect on the life of the crofters, who went on growing their crops and herding their cattle and worrying about the weather and the tides. They had suffered badly under the Danes, and must have welcomed more peaceful times, and the rebuilding of Columba's monastery on Iona; but the Benedictine monks were different from the Celtic monks, more concerned with their own Order and less interested in the lives of the people. So the crofters went on singing their own traditional songs in Gaelic. The main threat to their traditions did not come until the sixteenth century, when John Knox (1513–72) brought Calvinism to Scotland.[55] St Andrews on the east coast of Scotland was his centre for the dissemination of the Geneva doctrines, and the effect on the Western Isles seems to have been patchy. Though statues and crucifixes were smashed or burned, relics scattered and stained-glass windows broken, the new zealots would have approved of the use of the vernacular, and the emphasis the Islanders placed on the Bible, particularly the Psalms. When the conflict was finally resolved, Lewis and Harris had come largely under the influence of the Free Presbyterian Church of Scotland, or 'Wee Frees', while Barra at the other end of the chain was largely Roman Catholic.

Despite all these changes, the old songs, relics of an undivided Christendom embellished with local folklore, continued to be sung on the Isles as the crofters worked, even if they had to croon them under their breath.

Part 2

gaelic songs

Note

The number at the end of each poem gives the reference (volume and page) to the Oliver and Boyd edition of *Carmina Gadelica*. In each case, the reference is to the English translation. The Gaelic version is given on the facing page. In the footnotes, *CG* refers to the same edition.

1
the powers of heaven

God of the Moon

God of the moon, God of the sun,
God of the world, God of the stars,
God of the waters, the land, the skies,
Who sent us the King of promise.

Mary knelt to do your will,
Her child was born, the King of Life,
Darkness and tears were left behind,
And the bright star rose to guide us.

It shone on the land, it shone on the sea,
On storm and calm at the water's edge,
Grief was no more, and joy prevailed,
And the world was filled with music.

[*CG* 2.167]

This poem celebrates in a few words the Creation of the universe, God's re-demptive act in the incarnation of his Son Jesus Christ, and the daily guid-ance of the Holy Spirit. The Islanders live in 'storm and calm at the water's edge' under the lights of heaven.

He Lit the Stars

He lit the stars
On the crests of the clouds,
And the choirs of heaven
    Praise him.

Christ came down
With the Father's love;
Angels and saints
    Praise him.

Christ my beloved,
Son of Mary,
Night and day
    I praise you.

[*CG* 1.45]

The Islanders would have seen the stars as fixed points in the heavens. Moonlight and starlight would have been their only means of navigation after dark.

Hey, the Gift

Hey, the gift, ho, the gift,
The gift to all mankind.

Son of the dawn, Son of the clouds,
Son of the world, Son of the stars,
Son of the rain, Son of the dew,
Son of the firmament, son of the sky,
Son of the flame, Son of the light,
Son of the elements, Son of the heavens,

Son of the moon, Son of the sun.
Son of Mary, obedient to God,
Son of God, and good news to us,

Hey, the gift, ho, the gift,
The gift to all mankind.

[*CG*1.141]

There are strong parallels here with the Benedicite Omnia Opera – '*O all
ye works of the Lord, bless ye the Lord', the song of Shadrach, Meshach and
Abed-nego in the Book of Daniel 3.57–90. The monks would have said or
chanted this canticle at Mattins, the first service of the day.*

The Power of Life

Jesus cursed the fig-tree,
Had it been his will,
He could have brought it back to life
In leaf and bloom and fruit.

Every plant that grows in earth,
Every life-form on the shore,
Every creature in the sea,
Every creature in the stream,
Every creature in the sky,
Every bird upon the wing,
Every star which shines above
Proclaims his mighty power.

[*CG*1.39]

*This poem, based on the biblical story of Christ's cursing of the fig tree (Matt.
21.19–20; Mark 11.12–14), celebrates the ultimate mystery of living organisms
and natural growth.*

The Trinity

The Three who are over me,
Above and below me,
In the earth and in the air,
In the great and pouring sea,
And in the heavens above.

[*CG* 3.93]

The pre-Christian traditions of the Islanders included the recognition of three as a sacred number. Their Christian faith shows no evidence of controversies over the Person of Christ – such as the Arian, Monophysite or Nestorian heresies, which caused conflict and division elsewhere in Christendom.

The Sun

Great sun of all the seasons,
As you traverse the skies,
Your path is strong on the wings of heaven,
Mother of the stars.

Swallowed by the ocean,
Undamaged, undefiled,
You rise on the peaceful waves again
Like a royal maiden in bloom.

[*CG* 3.311]

The apparent destruction of the sun by the waves in the west every evening, and its reappearance at dawn in the east, must have seemed like a daily mystery – and a miracle. In a pre-Copernican world, the Islanders would have assumed that the earth was fixed in space, and would not have known that it was round – though a thoughtful man who watched a fairly large ship disappear over the horizon hull first might have had his suspicions that it was at least curved.

The Virgin and Child

Behold the Virgin coming,
The young Christ at her breast.

O Mary Virgin! O Holy Son!
Bless this house, and all herein.
Bless our food and bless our board,
Bless the food, the flocks, the store.

When our food supplies ran low,
You, Lady, were our Mother, too,
Brighter than the waxing moon,
Rising over mountains steep,
Brighter than the summer sun
Shining joyously above.

On the doorstep here I stand,
Arise and open, in God's name.
Since your bard must leave you now,
Fill his bag with alms and gifts.

[*CG* 1.145]

The travelling bard ends his praise of the Virgin Mary with a request for alms. He would have been begging for food and drink, or for clothing produced in the croft.

Queen of Grace

Smooth her hand,
Fair her foot,
Graceful her form,
Winning her voice,
Gentle her speech,
Stately her bearing,
Warm her approach,
Mild her regard.

As the black-headed gull
Rides gently the waves,
So her lovely white breast,
Gently rises and falls.

Holy, the virgin of gold-mist hair,
Clasps her child at the mountain foot,
Alone they dwell under the arch of the sky,
No shelter or food to sustain them.

But God the Son is with her,
His mighty shield protects her,
His inspiration guides her,
His saving Word is food to her,
His bright star leads her on.
To her, darkness at night
Is like brightness at noon,
Each day is all joy,
To the Mary of Grace.

Wherever she goes
Throughout his creation,
The seven Beatitudes
Are holding her fast.

[*CG* 2.209]

The Virgin Mary is the human Mother of God, but the Child she holds in her arms is eternal. She is already inspired and protected by him, though his earthly life lies ahead on her timescale. She is also the chief of the saints in heaven, who can be invoked to help men and women in times of need. The Beatitudes (Matt. 5.3–11) are nine in number in modern biblical texts; but the Islanders would only have known the Bible through the early translations available to the monks. Seven, like three, was a number of traditional power.

The Cross of the Saints

The cross of the saints and the angels be with me
From the top of my head to the edges of my soles.

Michael and glorious Mary,
Gentle Bride of the locks of gold,
Preserve me in my weakly body,
Keep me on the righteous path.

I am weak and poor in spirit.
Keep me from sin,
Keep me from harm,
Shield me tonight.

[*CG* 1.47]

Poor in spirit: Alexander Carmichael's translation of choich-anama bhochd *is 'soul-shrine poor'; but 'soul' in Scots dialect means 'spirit' in English. The reference is probably to the opening words of the Sermon on the Mount (Matt. 5.3).*

Michael Militant

Michael the warrior,
King of the angels,
Shield all your people
By the power of your sword.

Spread your wings
From east to west,
Over land and sea,
Shielding us from the foe.

Be with us on our journey
And in the battle's heat,
Until we reach the river
Ahead of us at last.

[*CG* 3.145]

The archangel Michael's feast day is 29 September, Michaelmas Day. Biblical references to him are limited to the Book of Daniel (Dan. 10.13, 21; 12.1), a brief reference in the General Epistle of Jude (verse 9) and the account of the War in Heaven in the Revelation of St John the Divine (Rev. 12.7). Michael is the messenger who takes the soul at the moment of death to present it before Christ. The river ahead is the Jordan, a synonym for death.

The Shield of Michael

Michael the victorious,
I live beneath your shield.

Michael of the white steed,
Michael of the flashing blade,
Conqueror of the dragon fierce,
Ranger of the heavens,
Warrior of the King of all,
Guard my back.

On the machair, on the meadow,
On cold and heathery hill,
If I should cross the oceans
And travel the whole world,
No harm could ever come to me
With Michael as my aid.

My horses and my cattle,
My flocks of woolly sheep,
The crops in field or ripened sheaves,
My stores and all my goods,
All these blessings come from God,
And Michael keeps them safe.

[*CG* 1.209]

'*Machair*': machera, *wide sandy strips by the sea in the Outer Hebrides.*

The Ancestry of Brigid

This is the line of descent of Bride,
Radiant flame of gold,
Bride the daughter of Dugall the brown
Son of Aodh, son of Art,
Son of Con, of Crear son,
Son of Cis, son of Cormac,
Son of Carruin.

Every day and every night,
I recite the family tree of Bride,
I shall live, and not be killed,
I shall be safe, and never harried,
I shall be free, not shut in a cell,
I shall be whole, and not be maimed,
Christ will remember me.

No fire, no sun, no moon shall burn me,
No lake, no river, no sea shall drown me,
No evil fairy dart shall harm me,
Holy Mary shall protect me,
And my foster-mother, Bride.

[CG1.175]

The line 'Brigid, excellent woman, golden flame' occurs in the Félire *of Oengus the Culdee, who died in 824 according to Irish chronicles.*

According to Brigid's ninth-century chronicler, Cogitosus, Brigid's father was named Dubthach; but the genealogies recited by bards and travelling musicians were not necessarily accurate in detail.

St Brigid's Aid

Brigid of the mantles,
Brigid of the peat-heap,
Brigid of the twining hair,
Brigid, woman seer,

Brigid of the white feet,
Brigid of the calm,
Brigid of the white hands,
Brigid of the cows,

Brigid, my companion,
Brigid, nurse of Christ,
Every day and every night,
I list your proud descent.

I shall not die in battle,
I shall not be gashed and torn,
I shall not be despoiled,
For Christ will be my aid.

No sun shall scorch me,
No fire shall burn me,
No sea shall engulf me,
No river shall drown me,
No bad dreams shall haunt me,
No spells be cast over me,
Saint Mary shall keep me,
And Brigid, my friend.

[CG 3.157]

Columba Says . . .

Columba says that those who give
In kindness to the needy
Will have a right to God, unlike
The liars and the greedy;

For those who swear against the truth
And those who steal from neighbours
Shall go to hell, shall go to hell,
In spite of all their labours.

[CG 2.169]

Columba and the White Cow

Come now, O Columba,
And heal my dear white cow.
Come now, O Columba,
For she is water-sick.

How so, O thick-tressed woman,
Am I to heal your cow,
With one foot in the coracle
And the other foot on shore?

Columba came up to the knoll,
And laid hands on the cow,
And healed it in the name of God,
Lord of eternity.

[CG 4.289]

Columba travelled from island to island to visit his monks at their mission stations. This picture of him on Mull 'with one foot in the coracle and the other foot on shore', stopping to heal an old woman's one cow, is typical of many anecdotes told about him. Alexander Carmichael was told, 'There was no one like Calum Cille, no one, my dear. He was big and handsome and eloquent, haughty to the over-haughty and humble to the humble, kind, kind to the weak and the wounded.'

Guardians

Holy Apostles, guard me,
Holy angels, guard me,
Quiet Brigid, guard me,
Gentle Mary, guard me,
Warrior Michael, guard me.

God of the elements, guard me,
Christ the loving, guard me,
Holy Spirit, guard me,
Shield me, keep me safe.

[*CG* 3.107]

2
home and family

The Beltane Blessing

True and bountiful Trinity,
Bless me, my wife and children,
My tender children and their beloved mother.

All that I own,
On mountain or plain,
Cows and crops, sheep and corn,
From Hallow Eve to Beltane Eve,
Progress with gentle blessing,
From sea to sea and river mouth,
From wave to wave and waterfall.

May the Trinity hold my possessions,
May the Trinity guard me in truth,
Satisfy my soul with the words of Paul,
And shield my loved ones
Beneath the wing of glory.

Bless everything and everyone
In this little household of mine,
May Christ's cross keep us in love
Till we see the land of joy.

When the cattle leave their stalls,
When the sheep forsake the fold,
When the goats go up to the mountains of mist,
May the Holy Spirit tend them.

Morning and evening
This I pray,
God who created me
Hear my prayer.

[CG 1.183]

Hallow Eve to Beltane Eve: through the months of winter, when the cattle,
sheep and goats were penned. All Hallows is All Saints Day, 1 November. The
pre-Christian festival of Beltane and the lighting of the new fire took place
about the beginning of May.

The Rock of Rocks

On the Rock of rocks
The peace of Peter and Paul,
Of James and John the beloved
And of the pure perfect Virgin.

The peace of the Father of joy,
The peace of the Christ of suffering,
The peace of the Spirit of grace
To us and our children.

[CG 1.43]

St Peter and St Paul are invoked together. This was common practice in the
early Church, although we know from the Acts of the Apostles that the two
had major disagreements, and did not work together. They share a feast day,
29 June. Here and elsewhere, St James is invoked as a single person, though
there were two Apostles of that name – James son of Zebedee and brother of
John (St James the Great), and James the son of Alphaeus (St James the Less).
St John is 'the Beloved Disciple'.

God Shield the House

God shield the house, the fire, the cows,
And all who sleep herein.
This night, preserve all those I love
From violence and harm.

Save us from our enemies
May Mother Mary's Son
Protect us while we take our rest
This night, and nights to come.

[*CG* 1.101]

The preservation of the fire through the night was so important – and the risk of fire so great – that it was natural to pray for God's protection in that respect, as for the house, the cattle and the family.

House Peace

The peace of God, the peace of men,
The peace of Columba kind,
The peace of Mary, mother mild,
The peace of Christ the King,
Be on each window, on each door,
Upon each hole that lets in light,
On the four corners of my house,
On the four corners of my bed.
On every thing my eyes shall see,
On every scrap of food I eat,
Upon my body, bound to earth
Upon my soul that came from God.

[*CG* 3.265]

The reference to 'each hole that lets in light' suggests that the windows were fairly rudimentary – no more than holes in the walls. Though glass was produced in Syria a century before the birth of Christ, glazed windows were comparatively rare in Europe until the fifteenth century, and would have been unknown in the Isles. Possibly the more elaborate houses had shutters to keep out the wind and the rain. There would have been a hole in the roof to let out the smoke from the fire.

House Blessing

God bless the house
From site to stay,
From beam to wall,
From end to end,
From ridge to floor,
From balk to roof-tree,
From found to summit.

[*CG* 1.105]

A balk was a beam or rafter. The Eastern Orthodox Church has a much larger number of sacraments than the Western Church and one of them is the laying of a corner-stone or foundation stone for a new house. This prayer may have been used in the same way, to bless the start of a new construction.

The Aid-Woman's Prayer

Behold, O Mother Mary,
This woman near to death,
And Jesus, Son of Mary,
Have mercy on her now.
Give her rest from labour
And bring the child to life.

Dear Christ, look upon her,
Deliver her from death,
You alone possess the power,
You only are the King of health,
Let the little vine-shoot rest
And give its mother peace.

[*CG* 4.193]

The birth of a child must have been a frequent event in the Islanders' small homes, and sometimes a very painful and dangerous one for the mother. This poem would have been chanted or sung by the 'aid-women' helping the mother. The 'little vine-shoot' is the child, struggling for existence.

Childbirth

Come to my aid
Sweet Mary and Bride,
As Anna bore Mary,
As Eile bore John Baptist,
As Mary bore Christ,
And perfect he was
From quickening to birth.

Help me bear this child,
Help me bring it to life,
Great is my travail,
Help me, O Bride.

[CG 1.177]

This poem would have been chanted by the woman in labour. 'Anna' is St Anne, mother of the Virgin Mary. 'Eile' is St Elizabeth, mother of John the Baptist. St Brigid (Bride) was widely known in Ireland and the Isles as 'the Aid-woman' because of her skill in midwifery. When legends about her proliferated, she was sometimes said to have been the wife of the innkeeper in Bethlehem, thought to have assisted in the birth of Christ – though this must have been difficult to reconcile with her Irish ancestry.

Blessing the New Child

One drop for the Father,
One drop for the Son,
One drop for the Spirit,
Small beloved one,

To keep you from all evil,
To hold and keep you free,
To shield you and surround you,
To save you for the Three.

[CG 3.7]

This was probably a form of conditional baptism administered as soon as the umbilical cord had been cut, and the child washed. Weakly babies must have been common. Many would not have survived long enough to be taken to church and ritually baptised in the way described in the following poem. Traditionally, nurses and midwives have long carried out a similar emergency baptism procedure for a weakly child in order to give it a name.

Baptism

God of the heights,
Come down to this child
The child of my body,
Bless him today.

When the priest of the King
Pours water upon him,
Holy Trinity, bless him
And give him your grace.

Guide him on his journey,
Make him honest and strong,
With the wisdom of angels,
So when his life is done,
He can stand in your presence
Without blame or reproach.

[*CG* 1.115]

Bathing the Baby

A scoop of water for your age,
A scoop to make you grow,
A scoop of water for your mouth,
And lovely things to eat.

You shall have dainties,
Crowdie and kail,
You shall have your share
Of honey and milk.

You shall have your share
Of butter and whey,
Yellow eggs at Easter,
And meat from the hunt.

You shall have your share
Of tribute and gifts,
You shall have your share,
Of hunting and chase.

You shall have your share
Of ruling and palaces,
And your share of Paradise,
My little love.

[*CG* 1.61]

The last two verses were presumably sung only to a baby of noble birth. Crowdie is a soft cheese, traditionally made from curds and butter. Kail is a broth made from greens. Food must often have been scarce in the winter, and there were many mouths to feed. The baby was being assured that its needs would not be forgotten.

Poem for a Young Bride

I wash your hands
In flowing wine,
In the lustral fire
Of the seven elements,
In raspberry juice
And flowing honey.

May your pretty young face
With graces be crowned:
The grace of form,
The grace of virtue,
The grace of good fortune,
The grace of wisdom,
The grace of chastity,
The grace of charity,
The grace of kind speech.

Unknown is the place
To which you are going,
Unknown are the people
You'll meet there, brown swan.

Those people will love you,
Controlling their tongues
And never say cruel things
That cause you distress.

You'll be shade in the heat to them,
Shelter in cold,
Eyes to the sightless,
The pilgrim's stout staff.

You are an island
In the wild sea,
You are a fortress
In the bare land.

You are an oasis
In desert sands.
You are the health
That can cure the sick.

You are the happiness
Of all joyous things,
You are the light
Of the sun's shining rays.

The step of the deer on the hill,
The step of the horse on the plain,
The grace of the swan on the water,
The beauty of all good desires,
The glory of Christ our Lord,
Is in your purity.

May you have
The best hours of the day,
The best day of the week,
The best week of the year,
The best year God can give you.

Peter has come, and Paul has come,
James has come, and John has come,
Mary Virgin pure has come,
And Michael, chief of hosts,

And Jesus Christ himself has come,
The Holy Spirit of God has come,
The King of Kings directs your course
In love, to give you love.

[CG1.7]

The uneven rhythm of this long poem suggests that it is a collection of pieces to be sung to a young bride by the women who are preparing her for her wedding. She was probably a chief's daughter. There were many arranged marriages to forge alliances and consolidate property holdings, and she might not even have met her bridegroom. She would have needed all the support the women could give her. The 'brown swan' (eala dhonn) is a cygnet which has not yet grown the white feathers of adulthood.

A Son's First Hunt

Young son of my body, you go out to hunt,
And I must teach you how,
In the name of the Apostles
And of the Son of God,

In the name of Paul and Peter,
Of James, and Baptist John,
Of John Divine, physician Luke,
Of martyred Stephen, Muriel fair,
And Mary, mother mild,

In the name of holy Patrick,
Columba the beloved,
Of Adamnan, the monk of laws
And Brigid of the cows.

In the name of Michael,
Chief of heavenly hosts,
And of the great archangels,
Glorious above,

Do not kill the swimming duck,
Or her little brood,
Spare the lovely singing swan
And the water-fowl.
Spare their feathers, spare their lives,
While they tread the waves.

If you must kill, then always kill
Fowl upon the wing.
Do not eat fallen fish or flesh
Dead upon the ground.

Be thankful if you snare a bird
Though nine may swim away,
Mary will love you more for this,
And Bride will give you cows.

[*CG* 1.311]

One can imagine the young huntsman becoming somewhat restive during the long invocation which precedes these injunctions to sportsmanship. Fish or flesh found dead are to be avoided because they might be contaminated. Catching fowl upon the wing must have been difficult when the only means available were a bow and arrow; but the Islanders were not dependent on hunting, since every croft had its chickens, cows and sheep.

The (male) archangel Muriel appears in an apocryphal Jewish account of the death of Moses as receiving the prophet into heaven. Alexander Carmichael may have assumed that Muriel was female – a mistake perpetuated in some New Age accounts of angels.

Adamnan, ninth abbot of Iona, was renowned for drafting a law which spared women, young boys and monks from attack during tribal warfare.

A Prayer for the Dying

O God, this is a sinful woman,
In a body failing fast.
Tonight she cannot name her sins.
Keep her in your care.

Jesus Christ, you bought her soul.
When the time shall come
For the final reckoning,
Hold her in your hand.

May Michael, king of angels
Come to meet her soul.
Michael, come and lead it home
To the heaven of Christ above.

[*CG* 1.119]

Death, like birth, would usually have taken place in the crowded conditions of the family home. Even small children would have been familiar with both as regular events in the cycle of daily life.

Funeral Weather

The black wrath of God
Means grief for a soul which has sinned,
The white wrath of the King of stars
Means sadness for one who shunned good.

A perfect calm on sea and land,
Peace on moor and meadow,
Means God is joyful as he takes
The new soul to his care.

May the day of my death be bright,
A day of peace and joy,
May the hand of Michael hold me up
And save my soul at last.

[*CG* 3.369]

The archangel Michael is again represented as the heavenly messenger. Funerals in bad weather must have been particularly gloomy occasions, since the weather was thought to indicate divine disapproval of the person who had died.

3
work in the home

Kindling the Fire

I will kindle my fire this morning
In the presence of the angels of heaven,
Without malice, without jealousy, without envy,
Without fear, without terror
Of anyone under the sun,
With the Son of God to shield me.

God, kindle in my heart a flame
Of love for my neighbours and foes,
For my friends and all my kindred,
For the brave, for the knave, for the beggar,
O Son of the loveliest Mary,
From the lowliest creature there is
To the name that is highest of all.

[CG 1.231]

*The usual practice was to take a pan of glowing embers to start a new fire
from an existing one. The practice of lighting one fire from another was still
common in most places until the invention of matches and other combustible
materials.*

Banking the Fire

I will bank the fire
As Mary would do it.
Bride and Mary
Guard us tonight.

Who stands without?
Michael, radiant and strong.
Who guard the floor?
John and Peter and Paul.
Who stand by my bed?
Sun-bright Mary and her Son.

The mouth of God ordained it,
The angel of God proclaimed it,
An angel white to guard the fire
Until white day shall come.

[*CG* 1.237]

Peat fires could be banked up to smoulder very slowly during the night, to save 'borrowing fire' in the morning. The process of banking the fire, known as 'smooring' in Scotland, was a regular household ritual.

Milking Song

Come, Mary mild, and milk my cow,
Come, Bride, and hold her tight,
Come, Columba the benign,
Circle her with your arms.

Ho, my heifer, my gentle heifer,
Gentle, dear and kind,
For the sake of the King of kings
Take to your calf today.

Come, Mary Virgin, to my cow,
Come, Bride the splendid, come,
Put your arms beneath my cow,
Milkmaid of Jesus Christ.

[CG 1.271]

Many runes were sung to the cows. According to Alexander Carmichael, the cows became so used to this musical accompaniment that they would not give milk without crooning, and a milkmaid with a good voice was highly prized.

The Brown Cow

Give your milk, brown cow,
Give your milk, brown cow,
Give your milk, brown cow,
Heavily flowing.

My beloved shall get white-bellied calves
And a gentle halter round her legs,
Not made of hair or heather or lint,
But one brought here from Saxon land,
Oh ho! from Saxon land.

My beloved shall be safe from any harm,
On hill and heath and plain.
She shall have grass from pastures rich,
And the wine of the hills from steepest bens.
Oh ho! the steepest bens.

[CG 1.269]

Lint was a form of unworn linen from flax. It would be interesting to know what gentler form of tether was brought from 'Saxon land'. The use of this phrase suggests that the song dates from before the Norman Conquest – or alternatively, that news of the Norman Conquest had not reached the crofters.

Churning the Butter

Come with the free, come,
Come with the bound, come,
Come with the bells, come,
Come with the blade, come,
Come with the sharp, come,
Come with the hounds, come,
Come with the wild, come,
Come with the mild, come,
Come with the kind, come,
Come with the loving, come,
Come with the yellow butter
As the churn is turning.

The free will come,
The bound will come,
The bells will come,
The blades will come,
The sharp will come,
The hounds will come,
The wild will come,
The mild will come,
The kind will come,
The loving will come.

The golden butter will come to the brim
As the churn is turning.

A splash is here,
A plash is here,
A crash is here,
A squash is here,
A big soft snail is here,
The yield of the cows is here,
Lumps yellow and fresh,

Finer than honey,
Better than wine,
Soft and fair and full.

Come poor, come naked, beggar come,
Come each hungry creature here,
And satisfy your thirst.

The God of the elements gave us milk,
Come, churn, come,
Fair-white Mary, prosper my work,
Come, churn, come,
Bless my butter, lovely Bride,
Come, churn, come.

The churning made of Mary
In the fastness of her glen,
To decrease her milk,
To increase her butter,
Butter-milk to wrist,
Butter to elbow
Come, churn, come.

[*CG* 2.145]

Anyone who has churned butter by hand will know that it is a seemingly end-less task. This long poem (here abridged) suggests the process by its rhythm and its many repetitions.

Columba's Butter Charm

The charm made by Columba
For a maiden in the glen,
To make her milk more plentiful
And her butter firm.

Come, butter lumps, come,
Come, butter lumps, come,

Come, rich lumps, masses large,
Come, butter lumps, come.

God who made the sun to shine,
Gave us food in crops and herd,
Put fish in the river, fish in the sea,
Make the butter come!

[*CG* 4.85]

Hatching the Chicks

I will rise early on Monday
To sing my rune and rhyme,
I will go sunwise, east to west,
My basket in my hand.

I will seek my hen's warm nest,
My left hand to my breast,
My right hand held across my heart,
To ask the help of God
Who gave us of his grace
In fields and farm and flocks.

I will close my two eyes,
And slowly move along,
As in a game of blind man's buff,
To find my hen's warm nest.

The first egg which I take out
I circle widdershins,
Two more eggs come to join it,
So three lie in my trug.

Up goes my right hand smoothly
Three more are lifted out.
I send a prayer to God above
To give me six, all sound.

Up goes my left hand also
In the name of Christ the King.
When I have ten, I seek two more
From the breast of the speckled hen,

Then my clutch will be complete.
In silence I will go
To mark the ends of each with soot,
In the name of God above,
Creator of the sea and hill,
In the name of all the saints
And of apostles twelve,

And in Columba's name, I'll choose
To set in line my batch
On Thursday next, Columba's day,
On Friday they will hatch.

[*CG* 1.285]

*Every croft would have had its own hens, and they would have been the house-
wife's responsibility. 'Widdershins' is an anti-clockwise movement, against
what appears to be the course of the sun, designed to frustrate the forces of
evil. Thursday was Columba's day. The eggs for hatching were marked with
soot to distinguish them from the eggs for cooking.*

· Parching the Corn

If the flame burns grey and slender,
Curving from the peat,
Or if it leaps out sharp and fierce,
I will not parch my corn.

Corn ears must be parched gently
Over steady fire and slow,
Fragrant fire and peaceful
To save the precious ears.

Parch, my corn ears, smoothly,
To feed my little child,
In the name of Christ the King,
Master of the elements,
Who gave us corn and bread to eat,
And broke and blessed our food.

[*CG* 1.251]

A quick way of preparing a small quantity of corn for bread or gruel was to dry it out in a bag of woven straw or grass hung over a peat fire. This was called 'parching' and produced bread with a strong flavour of peat.

The Warping Chant

Thursday is the day to start,
Blessed Thursday,
For sorting and teasing and washing the wool,
Combing and carding and dyeing and weaving.

A hundred and fifty strands to place,
Blue and scarlet and madder rose,
Two of white to match the blue,
Laid even side by side.

Bless me and mine, O gracious God,
Father of us all,
Christ, shepherd of the human flock,
And Holy Spirit kind.

Mary fair, look down from heaven,
Archangel Michael strong,
Bestow your grace and wisdom true
On all beneath this roof.

Ward off every evil eye,
Ward off those who mean us harm,
Consecrate the warp and woof
Of every thread.

Put your arms around us now,
Each woman in her task,
Help us in our time of need
As we make the cloth.

Plants and beasts and humankind
Owe their growth to you,
Give us grass for the sheep, and innocent lambs,
To help the flocks to grow.

From the sheep, we take the wool
And nourishing milk to drink.
We shall have food, and we shall have cloth,
This day and every day.

[*CG* 1.295]

This poem expresses very clearly the many separate tasks involved in turn-ing wool from the sheep into cloth. Again, 'Columba's Thursday' is cited as the day to start. The women probably sang as they worked: the metre of the original suggests the thump of the loom. The final verses express their under-standing of the whole process of plant and animal growth.

Loom Blessing

Every colour in the rainbow
Has gone through my fingers
Beneath the Cross of Christ,
Every thread to the loom.

White and black, red and rose,
Green, dark grey and scarlet,
Blue and dappled and colour of sheep,
And every thread in its place.

I beseech calm Bride the generous,
I beseech mild Mary loving,
I beseech Christ the compassionate,
That I may not die without them,
That I may not die without them.

[CG 1.301]

Consecration of the Cloth

Well can I say my rune,
Descending in the glen,
One rune, two runes,
Three runes, four runes,
Five runes, six runes,
Seven and a half runes.

When the man who wears this cloth
Goes to battle, let him not
Be torn in flesh or wounded sore.
May God be his shield.

Green cresses from beneath a stone,
Deer's shank and herring's head,
Speckled salmon's tail, combine
In this secret spell.

This is newly-woven cloth,
Not second-hand and worn,
Never has it been the right
Of priest or sacristan.

[*CG*1.309]

The CG translation describes the cloth as 'not thigged'. 'Thigged' is a Scottish
dialect term which implies 'genteel begging'. 'Second-hand and worn' seems
appropriate; but the last two lines suggest that new cloth may have been made
into habits or ecclesiastical vestments for the monks, and later cut up to pro-
vide clothes for children. The following poem suggests a similar practice.

A New Suit for a Son

This is not second-hand cloth,
I did not beg it,
No priest possessed it,
No pilgrim wore it.

It is yours, my son,
Newly made, I swear,
As God is my judge,

Enjoy it, wear it,
Until you find it
In shreds and strips,
In tatters and rags!

[*CG*4.99]

63

The Lord's Day

The Lord's Day, the seventh day
God ordained for rest,
To bring us to eternal life
In the strength of Jesus Christ.

There shall be no labour
Of man or ox or beast,
No spinning and no weaving,
No sowing, harrowing, reaping,
No rowing, games or fishing,
No hunting, arrow-trimming,
No cleaning byres,
No threshing corn,
No grinding in the mill.

No weeping on the Lord's Day,
No tears, no cries, no sobbing,
Let the women keep their peace
Till dawn of Monday's light.

No strong drink on the Lord's Day,
Water will cure your ills,
Gather no kindling, lest the flame
Lie quiet till Monday noon.

Search not the hills for lamb or kid,
Do not mate cow and bull,
Keep your boat moored close by the shore,
And have no speech with strangers.

Who shall keep the Lord's Day
Shall find it calm and still
From setting sun on Saturday
Till Monday's rising sun.

[*CG* 1.217]

This sounds more like a set of Calvinist strictures than the relatively easygoing practices of the early Celtic Church; but Alexander Carmichael insists that he heard other poems on similar lines which could be traced back to the eighth century. If this is so, Sabbatarianism in the Isles has a very long history. In Celtic society, as in many Eastern societies, it was usual to hire mourners to weep for the dead, and the prohibition against weeping and sobbing women may have applied to them rather than to the women of the house.

4
the croft

Brigid's Charm

Whenever kindly Bride went forth,
Leaving her home, or coming home,
She put a charm on her goats and sheep,
On her horses, and on her cows,

To keep them from the rocks and cliffs,
From each other's heels and horns,
From surly hawk and raven swift,
From the eagle's deadly claws,

From the crafty, wily fox,
From the prowling hungry wolf,
From the pole-cat's hateful stink,
From the restless bear,

From all four-footed beasts with hooves
And every hatched with wings.

[CG 2.35]

*St Brigid's work covered a wide area. She usually drove herself in a small
chariot, and was a welcome visitor at many humble homes.*

The Fox

The spell of the wood-dog
On the feet of the fox,
On his heart, on his liver,
On his greedy gullet,
On his sharp and pointed teeth,
And his stomach's sensuous curve.

Hither and thither, the charm of Christ,
Kindly-white and milk-white,
The charm of Mary, tender-fair,
Against all those who harm the sheep,
Four-footed, winged or human.

[*CG* 2.129]

Foxes are shown in many folk stories as wily, intelligent and dangerous. They generally attacked chickens and lambs. Cattle, which were pastured higher on the hill or mountain slopes in summer, were at risk from wolves.

Guarding the Flocks

May mild Mary keep the sheep,
May Bride the tranquil keep the sheep,
May Columba keep the sheep,
May Maelrubba keep the sheep,
May Cormac keep the sheep,
From the fox and the wolf.

May Oran keep the kine,
May Modan keep the kine,
May Donnan keep the kine,
May Moluag keep the kine,
May Maelruan keep the kine,
On soft land and hard land.

May the Spirit keep the flocks,
May Mary's Son preserve the flocks,
May the God of Glory keep the flocks,
From wounding and from death-loss,
From wounding and from death-loss.

[*CG* 1.281]

All the saints named are known in the records of the early Celtic Church. Maelruan (died 792) was abbot of Tallaght, near Dublin. There are several Cormacs, but this one was probably Columba's friend and colleague; which would place his life in the second half of the sixth century. Oran was a monk of Iona. Modan may be Modomnoc, an Irishman of Columba's clan, the Uí Neill, who studied under St David at Menevia in Wales in the late sixth century. Donnan or Donan was the abbot of Eigg, martyred with his monks in a Danish raid in 618. Moluag of Lismore was a missionary to the Isles, thought to have been born in the south of Ireland, who died about 592. Maelrubba (642–722) was born in Ireland, studied in the missionary college at Benn Chorr (the Irish Bangor), and settled in Wester Ross, facing Skye.

Herding

The flock shall go before me
As Christ our King ordained,
And Bride herself shall keep them
On hill and glen and plain.

Arise now, Bride the gentle,
Fair and lovely Bride,
Keep my sheep from straying,
And save them from all harm.

From rocks, from drifts, from water
From crooked paths and pits,
From envy and from malice
And slender fairy darts.

Tend the lambs, O Mother Mary,
While Bride shall guard my flocks,
And powerful, kind Columba
Shall multiply my herds.

[*CG*1.275]

'Fairy darts' were not necessarily of supernatural origin: this was a name for
flint-headed arrows.

Columba's Herding

May the herding of Columba
Help you going and coming
On valley and hill, in regions rough,
From pit and mire and hill and crag,
From loch, and down the mountain side,
In dusk, and in the dark.

May the herding of Columba
Keep you from destruction,
Keep you from falling,
Keep phantoms at bay.

May the peace of kind Columba
Guard all your flock when grazing,
May Bride watch all your grazing,
Mary be with your grazing
And bring you safely home.

[CG 4.47]

Marking the Lambs

My knife will be new and shining and clean
To make the first of cuts
On a new male lamb that is blemish-free
While I kneel upon my plaid.

The first cut goes from east to west,
The second with the sun,
The lamb will go off with the blood flowing free
To graze upon the plain.

If the blood stays on the heather top
As froth, all will be well.
My flock will prosper without flaw
And clearly bear my mark.

May the Three in the city of glory above
Powerful blessings send
In heat and cold, from pasture to fold,
To guard my sheep and kine.

[CG 1.289]

Like the lifting of eggs for hatching, the marking of the lambs was a very ancient ritual, and the practice was a necessary one: Alexander Carmichael quotes estimates that there were over 250 different marks on Benbecula alone in his time, and more than 500 on South Uist, so the identification of lambs was important. The small native sheep – 'picturesque little animals' – were almost free of the diseases which affected sheep imported from the mainland.

Shearing the Sheep

Go shorn, and come woolly,
Bear me a lamb in the spring,
Bride endow you,
Mary sustain you,
Michael shield you

From the evil dog and the fox,
From the wolf and the cunning bear,
From the talons of the birds,
From the talons of the birds
With fiercely curving beaks.

[*CG* 1.293]

After shearing, this rune was recited as the sheep was set free and sent on its way. Eagles and buzzards were particular hazards for newborn lambs.

71

Pasturing the Cattle

Pastures long and smooth and wide,
Grassy meads beneath your feet,
May Christ Jesus be your friend,
May he bring you safely home
To the field of the fountains.

Closed be every pit to you,
Smoothed be every slope to you,
May the winds be kind to you
Beside the cold mountains.

Peter and Paul watch over you,
James and John watch over you,
Bride and Mary care for you,
Oh! The care of all the saints
Protect and strengthen you.

[*CG*1.279]

Calving

Come, Brendan, from the ocean,
Come, Ternan, powerful, strong,
Come, Michael, bright and valiant,
And help my cow to bear;
And help my cow to take her calf
In the name of the High King.
Come, beloved Colum,
Come, Bride, and Mary fair,
And help my cow to take her calf,
The heifer of my love.

The stock-dove will come from the wood,
The tusk will come from the sea,
The fox will come friendly from forest lair,
To hail my cow, my lovely cow,
The heifer of my love.

Hey, my heifer, ho, my heifer,
Heifer of my love.

[*CG*1.259]

Brendan is St Brendan the Navigator, whose ocean voyages became a cele-brated medieval romance. Colum is St Columba. Ternan is St Ternan, one of his monks on Iona. The 'tusk' is presumably a walrus. Seals are more common in the Isles, but have no tusks.

When the Tide Flows In

When the sea is full and the tide flows in,
With gentle Mary's aid,
I shall pluck the figwort
To make my cattle yield.

By the power of kindly Colum,
By Oran's holy strength,
By Bride, the best of women,
My cows shall give of their milk.

The King of kings ordained it,
The Being of life ordained it,
In badger and reindeer, sow and mare,
In heifer and deer, in ewe and goat,
In breast and gland, in udder and teat,
The milk should plenteously flow.

There shall be milk and butter,
And cream for our delight,
The cows shall calve, the calves shall feed
In nature's joyous round.

May no harm come near them
In the name of God
And his holy Mother
And Patrick, our good saint.

[CG 2.87]

Though St Columba's original buildings were destroyed in Danish raids in the ninth century, the ground plan is known, and the reconstituted oratory or chapel of St Oran stands next to the abbey.

Ditch of Mary

Ditch of Mary,
Ditch of Mary,
Heron legs,
Heron legs,
Ditch of Mary,
Heron legs under you,
Safe passage before you.

Mary placed a branch in it,
Bride gave a hand to it,
Columba placed his foot in it,
Patrick placed a stone.

Ditch of Mary,
Ditch of Mary,
Heron legs under you,
Safe passage before you.

[CG 2.133]

When a cow hesitated to cross a channel or a wide ditch, the driver would throw a stalk or twig into the water to persuade her that it was safe to cross. Any stalk could be used, except the reed, or any twig except one from the aspen tree, or yjr thorn, because all three had associations with Christ's Crucifixion. For poems on the Aspen and the Reed, see Section 8. The cow was being urged to breach the water like a heron, a long-legged wading bird.

The Hide Disease

Teasel to tease you,
Comb to comb you,
Card to card you,
Cat to scratch you,
In dole and in dolour.

An old yellow cat,
Purring and taloned,
To scratch the disease off
Your poor shrivelled hide.

In peace and in comfort,
Full of marrow and sap,
Full of tallow and fat,
Full of strength and power,
Full of blood and flesh,
May you be.

In the name of the Being,
Creator of men,
And also Creator
Of a poor hidebound cow.

[*CG* 4.311]

The Hide Disease caused the skin of the cow to dry and crack. It could sometimes be cured by plant extracts, but the more efficient method was to 'scarify' the hide on the unfortunate animal's back. A cat, drawn by the tail, was often used for this purpose. The cow was tied to a stake and, maddened with pain, would 'lunge frantically with head and horns and hoof'. The process must have been equally unpleasant for the cat.

Sowing the Seed

I will go out and sow the seed
In the name of God who gave it growth.
I will stand and face the wind,
Throw a handful up on high.

Should a grain fall on stony ground
It shall surely die,
But grain which falls into the earth
Will flourish with the dew.

On Friday, the day for sowing,
Every seed which lies asleep
In the winter's icy grip
Will take root in the moistened earth,
Drawing life from dew and wind
As the King of the elements planned.

I will go from east to west
All about the field,
In the name of Ariel,
In the name of Gabriel,
In the name of angels nine
And of Apostles twelve.

Father, Son and Spirit,
Help the seed to grow,
Every seed on this my land
Till the harvest come.

On the feast of Michael
The first cut shall be made,
Round about the root I choose
My sickle sharp shall go.

Round my head it thrice shall whirl
While I face the sun,
Then, eyes closed, I'll throw it far
And watch how it shall land.

If it falls in a single bunch
The harvest will be good;
When the storms of winter blow
We shall have food to eat.

[*CG* 1.243]

Alexander Carmichael found that this ritual was still performed in the Isles at the end of the nineteenth century 'with great care and solemnity'. March and April were the sowing times, and St Michael and All Angels' Day, 29 September, was the traditional time for reaping.

Reaping the Harvest

May God bless my reaping,
Ridge and plain and field,
Every curve of sickle,
Every ear in sheaf.

Bless each son and daughter,
Wife and tender child,
Keep them safe beneath his shield,
Guarded by the saints.

Guard each goat and sheep and lamb,
Cow and horse and store of grain,
Safely guide my flocks and herds
To a place of rest.

In the name of Michael,
In the name of Bride,
In the name of Mary,
God's true branch of grace.

[*CG* 1.247]

The Flood

On Monday, the storm will come,
The great storm, rending the skies,
The elements raging across our land
And the people quiet with fear.

On Tuesday, the hail will come,
Icy, piercing hail,
Cutting our cheeks and staining our brows
With streams of wine-red blood.

On Wednesday will come the wind,
Scouring hill and plain,
Sharp and vicious in gales and gusts,
Thunder and lightning fierce.

On Thursday will come the rain
In drenching, blinding sheets,
Tearing the leaves from the quaking trees
And the people from their homes.

On Friday will come the dark,
The whole world overcast,
Branches and dead fish strewn around
And the weary people lost.

On Saturday comes the great wave,
The sea will invade the land,
The survivors will flee to the highest hills
In peril of their lives.

On Sunday, God will arise,
Almighty in his wrath;
He suffered pain upon the Cross,
We bear our crosses, too.

[CG 1.245]

This poem has many obscurities in the Carmichael version. Some of the words in the original are not listed in dictionaries, and may be specific to particular localities; but a very vivid picture comes through of the hazards and hardships of the crofters' lives. The sea was often a friend, but it could also become an enemy.

5

special occasions

Man of the Night

I am the Gift, I am the Poor,
I am the Man of the Night,
I am the Son of God at your door,
Asking gifts from you.

Bride the gentle cradled me,
Great Mary was my mother,
Here I stand, and bear my cross,
Open the door to me.

I see the hills, I see the shore,
And angels massed on high.
The dove of peace comes swiftly down,
Bringing the word of love.

[*CG* 1.143]

The word for gift (bannag) literally means a corn cake or bannock. The same word is used in 'Hey, the Gift', where Christ is the Gift to the human race. This mysterious and haunting poem was probably sung at Christmas by groups of 'guisers' asking for gifts of food, drink or clothing.

A Christmas Chant

Hail to the King, hail to the King,
Blessed is he, blessed is he.

Blest be this house and all herein,
Health and long life to all herein,
Hail to the King, hail to the King,
Blessed is he, blessed is he.

This is the night of Christ the King,
Born is the Son of Mary pure,
Hail to the King, hail to the King,
Blessed is he, blessed is he.

The soles of his feet have reached the earth,
Illumined the sun on the mountains high,
Hail to the King, hail to the King,
Blessed is he, blessed is he.

He shone on the earth, he shone on the land,
Shone on the wave as it beat on the shore,
Hail to the King, hail to the King,
Blessed is he, blessed is he.

Without beginning and end is he,
Throughout all time, to eternity,
Hail to the King, hail to the King,
Blessed is he, blessed is he.

[*CG* 1.127]

This is an abbreviated version of a long poem, of which there are numerous versions from different islands. The repetition of 'Hail to the King' (Ho Ri! or Ho Righ! in Gaelic) suggests that it was probably a processional, sung or chanted from croft to croft.

New Year's Eve

[*The mummers sing.*]

    Here we come to your door,
    To tell the generous wife
    That the New Year dawns tomorrow,
    And we are seeking gifts.

[*They gather round the fire, singing.*]

    May God bless this dwelling,
    Each stone and beam and stave,
    Good food and drink and clothing
    And good health be within.

[*If no gifts are forthcoming, they tramp loudly, shaking
the dust from their feet, and intoning maledictions.*]

    The curse of God be on you,
    The curse of the coming year,
    The mark of the crying buzzard,
    Of the raven and the eagle,
    And the mark of the sneaking fox.

    The mark of the dog be on you,
    Of the cat and the boar and the bear,
    The mark of the stinking polecat,
    And the mark of the prowling wolf.

[*CG* 1.157]

*Alexander Carmichael describes this as a song for 'Hogmanay' but the tradi-
tion of the 'guisers' or mummers who went from door to door on New Year's
Eve in the Isles may have been different from the Scottish Hogmanay. The
Gaelic word for the New Year is* Challaig.

New Year's Day

This first day of this new year
We never had before.
Let me use this gift of time
To praise your holy name.

Bless my eyes, that they may bless
All they see this day.
I will bless my neighbour, Lord,
Grant that he bless me.

God, give me an honest heart
Bless my wife and kin,
Bless our cattle, bless our home,
Watch over us always.

[CG 1.159]

Ash Eve

On Ash Eve
We shall have meat.
We should have that,
We should have that.

A slice of chicken,
Two bits of barley,
That is enough,
That is enough.

There will be mead,
There will be beer,
There will be wine,
That is our feast.

83

We shall have milk,
We shall have cream,
We shall have honey,
Plenty of that.

We shall have music,
Harp, lute and horn,
There will be melody,
Songs for the feast.

Bride will be with us,
Mary be with us,
Michael be with us,
Bright sword in hand,

Christ the King with us,
Spirit be with us,
Grace and peace with us,
Blessing our feast.

[*CG* 1.255]

Ash Eve is the day before Ash Wednesday, later called Shrove Tuesday: a day of feasting and celebration before the long Lenten fast. The wine may have been made from carrots or other locally grown plants. If it was grape wine, it probably came by sea from Spain or France along the sea routes. Spruce beer was a local product. Honey was particularly prized as a source of sweetness.

The Feast Day of Mary

On the feast day of Mary the fragrant,
Mother of the Shepherd King,
I cut me a handful of new corn,
And dried it in the sun.
I rubbed it sharply from the husk
With the flat palms of my hands.

I ground it in a quern on Friday,
I baked it on a fan of sheepskin,
I toasted it by a fire of rowan,
And I shared it with my kin.

I went sunwise round my dwelling,
In the name of Mary Mother,
Who promised to watch over me,
Who watches ever with me
All I possess, and in my soul
My purity of heart,
In daily work, in deeds of love,
In wisdom and in peace.

O Christ of grace and mercy,
Until my day of death,
You never will forsake me,
You never will forsake me.

[CG 1.195]

Sunwise: from east to west, the opposite of widdershins. The chief feast day of the Virgin Mary is 15 August, and this was the day for testing the new crop of corn, to be harvested six weeks later, on the day of St Michael and All Angels (29 September).

St Michael's Eve

Under this roof of mine
Herbs and roots and plants shall be
Mixed in the name of God the Son,
Who caused them all to grow.

Milk and eggs and butter,
The produce of the land,
Will keep us all in plenty,
Through the cold months to come.

Dandelion and garlic,
Herbs and spices too,
The three lovely flavours,
And Mary's special flower.

Make us to be humble,
Keep us all from harm,
Protect us all from evil,
Preserve us at all times,

In the name of Michael,
Angel of great power,
In the name of Christ the Lamb,
And Mother Mary mild,

Bless the produce of our hands,
Grant us to dwell in peace,
In the name of God the King,
Father of us all.

[*CG* 1.213]

The 'Struan' is the name of the corn cake baked on St Michael's Eve for the celebration to follow the first cutting of the corn on St Michael's Day. The rhythm of the poem suggests that it may have been said or sung while the cake mixture was being stirred. The garlic could be the flower of wild garlic, not the bulb. The Gaelic phrase translated here as 'the three special flavours' is tri ghroigeanan-cinn, *translated as 'the three carle-doddies' in CG. In Scottish dialect, carle-doddies are defined as grass-stalks, plantains and endearments or good wishes; but 'curlie-doddies', which include pine cones (pine nuts?), clover blossom (which contains honey) and plums, may perhaps have provided more suitable ingredients for a cake. 'Mary's flower' is the marigold.*

Sunday

Sunday is the holy day,
The day you owe to God.
Offer this day to all the world,
And your loving parents first.

Do not covet little or much,
Do not despise the weak,
Love the poor, shun evil deeds,
Lest they should earn you shame.

The Ten Commandments came from God,
Study them well, and know
You have the Word of God himself,
Not ikons to adore.

Be faithful to your Lord above,
In everything you do
Be true to him, and to yourself,
Whatever comes to you.

Do not be false to any man,
Lest men to you be false,
And though you travel earth and sea,
Walk in the steps of God.

[*CG* 1.223]

Sunday is to be a day of recollection and resolve for the coming week – a more positive attitude than that of the poem on 'The Lord's Day'. The CG *translation of* dhealbh *is 'ikons', but the reference is probably simply to the worship of images in general, rather than to the ikons of the Eastern Orthodox Church.*

Thursday

Day to send sheep to market,
Day to set cow on calf,
Day to put web in the warp,
The day of kind Columba.

Day to set out on the ocean,
Day to raise flag on staff,
Day to give birth and day to die,
Day to hunt on the heights,

Day to put horse in harness,
Day to send herds to pasture,
Day to make prayer be heard,
Day of Columba, Thursday,
Day of Columba, Thursday.

[*CG* 1.163]

There are many references in the poems to the importance of Thursday, which was considered specially auspicious for new ventures, and particularly devoted to St Columba, who is said to have been born and to have died on that day. Wednesday and Friday were fast days, which gave Thursday an added importance. Maundy Thursday, Diardaoin a brochain, or Gruel Thursday, was a day when offerings of mead, ale or gruel were made to the sea-gods, with a prayer for a plentiful harvest of seaweed to fertilize the crops. The ceremony was still carried out in Alexander Carmichael's time. He witnessed it, and commented, 'It shows the tolerant spirit of the Columban Church, and the tenacity of popular belief, that such a practice should have been in vogue so recently.'

Swans on Friday

I heard the sweet voice of the swans
Pouring forth their strength,
Singing on the wings of flight,
When day turned into night.

Silent I stood, and made no move,
And looked to see who led.
The graceful white swan flew in front,
The queen of fortune bright.

If you see a swan on Friday morn,
As night turns into day,
You know that you will prosper
Throughout the year to come.

But I saw my swans on Friday night,
And thought of how I lost
My goods and all my kinsfolk,
On Tuesday, a year ago.

[*CG* 2.183]

Days of the week, and even times of the day, were significant as being propitious or unpropitious. This sad little poem suggests that Tuesday was an unlucky day. Mornings were (as perhaps they are universally) times of optimism and hope, while evenings were times of reflection and sadness. The 'mute' white swan was thought to sing when it was dying.

6

the sea

Fishing

I will cast my hook, and catch a fish,
The first fish which I catch
Shall be for the poor, in the name of Christ,
Who calmed the winds and waves.

Ariel, Gabriel, Raphael kind,
Peter, Paul and John,
Kind Columba, friend to all
In their hour of need,

Mary mild and full of grace,
Be with us today,
Smooth the waves and bring our boat
To the fishing ground.

The Three on high protect us,
Christ's cross be our shield,
Till, all our journeys ended,
We reach the King of kings.

[*CG* 1.319]

There are some curious pre-Christian Irish traditions connected with fishing.
Alexander Carmichael describes a custom, still observed in his time, where-
by the young men would go out to fish on Christmas Day, and all the catch
would be given to widows, orphans and the poor as what was called Deride
Pheadair, *Peter's tribute.*

Master of the Waves

God the Father, God of power,
Jesus, Son of Sorrow,
Holy Spirit, Three in One,
Bless our boat today.

You brought Israel's children
Through the Red Sea's depths,
You brought your servant Jonah
From the belly of the whale.

On the Sea of Galilee
You calmed the angry waves,
Bringing Paul and all his friends
To safety on the shore.

Sanctify and shield us,
Master of the waves,
Take the helm,
Lead us in peace,
To our journey's end.

[CG 1.329]

St Paul was not on the Sea of Galilee with the disciples when Christ calmed the waves (Matt. 8.23–7; Mark 4.34–40; I Cor. 15.8), so Pol (Paul) in the Gaelic should presumably be Phedair (Peter); but this would spoil the rhythm of the chant, which was probably sung in time to the beat of the oars as the boat put out to sea.

Blest be the Boat

Helmsman:	Blest be the boat.
Crew:	God the Father bless her.
Helmsman:	Blest be the boat.
Crew:	God the Son bless her.
Helmsman:	Blest be the boat.
Crew:	God the Spirit bless her.
Chorus:	God the Father
	God the Son
	God the Spirit
	Bless the boat.
Helmsman:	What can befall you
	And God the Father with you?
Crew:	No harm can befall us.
Helmsman:	What can befall you
	And God the Son with you?
Crew:	No harm can befall us.
Helmsman:	What can befall you
	And God the Spirit with you?
Crew:	No harm can befall us.
Chorus:	God the Father
	God the Son
	God the Spirit
	With us eternally.
Helmsman:	What can you fear
	With the God of the elements over you?
Crew:	We are not afraid.
Helmsman:	What can you fear
	With the Christ of the elements over you?
Crew:	We are not afraid.
Helmsman:	What can you fear
	And the Spirit of the elements over you?
Crew:	We are not afraid.

Chorus:　　The God of the elements
　　　　　　The Christ of the elements
　　　　　　The Spirit of the elements
　　　　　　Close over us
　　　　　　Eternally.

[CG 1.333]

This sounds like a song for the crew of one of the larger sea-going vessels,
rather than the small coracles that plied the routes between the islands.

Ocean Blessing

God of the heights,
Give us your blessing,
Carry us safely
Over the sea
To a haven of peace.

Blest be our boat and our sturdy crew,
Blest be our anchors and our oars,
Travellers, stays and halyards all,
And the mainsails on our masts.

Order the elements kindly,
That we may go home in peace.
The Son of God will take the help
As he did for Columba kind.

Mary, Bride, Michael and Paul,
Peter, Gabriel, beloved John.
Make our faith to grow in us,
Based on the Rock of rocks.

> Seed of Adam though we be,
> Free us from death's bonds.
> Take us to the glorious land
> Where peace and mercy dwell.

[*CG* 1.325]

A 'traveller' in this context is the ring that holds the yardarm to the mast. Here St Paul figures again (mistakenly) as a fisherman, and saints and archangels are invoked together in a metre that matches the rhythm of the oars.

Ruler of the Elements

> God took the children of Israel
> By a path through the Red Sea,
> And quenched their thirst
> From an unhewn rock.
>
> Who stands at the tiller
> Speeding my boat?
> Peter and Paul and John the beloved,
> Honour and praise to them.
>
> Christ himself is at the helm,
> Steering in the wind from the south.
> Who calms the voice of the southern wind?
> Christ himself,
> Lord of saints,
> Son of Mary,
> Victorious.

[*CG* 1.331]

The biblical references are taken from Exodus 14.26–9 (the Israelites' crossing of the Red Sea) and Exodus 17.6 (Moses smiting the rock of Horeb). The Islanders were familiar with the Old Testament stories as well as with the Gospels.

No Crew of Landsmen

It was no crew of landsmen
Took the ferry out on Wednesday.
It is tidings of disaster
If they do not return,

What keeps you away?
Is it the angry sea
And the treacherous wind-gusts
That stop you from sailing?

Our one son went with them,
And three of my brothers,
And one of my nephews,
And, sorest of all,

My own man, my Donald.
I sit and sift ashes
And dig in the fields,
And weep in the glen.

For there is no laughter
Now the men have all gone,
No word of what happened,
Or if they will come back.

[*CG* 4.113]

It is said that 18 men of north St Kilda went to Boreray on an expedition to collect rams for their flocks. Like all the men of the Isles, they were experienced sailors. Storms kept them away for 18 weeks, and while they were away, the women, thinking them dead, mourned their loss.

The Cats are Come

The Cats are come on us,
The Cats are come on us,
The Cats are come on us,
They are come upon us.

To break in upon us,
To take spoil from us,
To steal the cows from us,
To cudgel our horses,
To strip bare our houses,
They are come upon us.

They are come, they are come,
They are come in the evil hour,
Here in among us,
Their stroke is upon us.

Sons of the wicked,
Come in tempest and storm,
Their blood on our meadows,
Their shafts by their sides
And their quivers well filled.

For murder and mauling,
For howling and hazard,
For pillage and plunder,
To steal cows in calving,
They are come.

In blood and in fury,
Weeping and screaming,
To take sheep from pasture,
Attacking on Thursday,
They are come upon us.

[CG 4.361]

These Cats were human marauders from the mainland, probably the men of Cataibh *(Sutherland). The Earl of Sutherland was known as the* Morair Chat, *the Lord of the Cat-folk. The fact that they attacked on Thursday, Columba's Day, was a particular insult.*

The Melodious Lady-lord

Who is the melodious lady-lord
At the base of the knoll,
At the mouth of the wave?

Neither duck nor swan is she,
No mavis, lark or merle on bough,
No murmuring ptarmigan,
No young salmon or seal is she,
No mermaid of the waves.
She does not spin, she plays no lyre,
Nor does she tend the sheep.

She is the daughter of a king,
Grand-daughter of a king,
Great grand-daughter of a king,
Great great grand-daughter of a king,
Great great great grand-daughter of a king,
Wife of a king,
Mother of a king,
Foster-mother of a king.
She sings softly to a king
Sheltering under her plaid.

From Erin she travelled
For Norseland bound,
May God travel with her
Wherever she goes.
[CG 2.203]

The mavis is the blackbird, and the merle or merlin a kind of small falcon. This poem is said to have been composed by two nuns who saw another nun, an Irish princess by birth, cradling a young king who had been driven out by a usurper. The child's mother and father had been killed, and the princess nun had been taking him to safety in Scandinavia. They were the only survivors of a shipwreck. The phrase 'lady-lord', bhain-tighearna, may imply that she was not only of noble birth: as the guardian of the young king, she held a position of authority. As she had been 'the wife . . . and mother of a king' she was presumably a widow who had followed the common custom of entering the religious life after the death of her husband. The nuns who discovered the pair on the beach and sheltered them are thought to have been members of a community attached to Iona.

Ebb and Flow

As it was
As it is
As it shall be
Evermore,
O Thou Triune
Of grace!

With the ebb
With the flow,
O Thou Triune of grace!
With the ebb
And with the flow.

[*CG* 2.217]

7

incantations

The Sign of God

I place this sign on your body,
The sign of the God of Life.
May he bring you health and wealth
And shield you safe from harm.

This is the sign that Mary
Put upon her Son:
Between sole and throat,
Between breast and knee,
Between back and breast,
Between chest and sole,
Between eye and hair.

Michael's host be with you,
His shield on your shoulder,
Nothing between heaven and earth
Can defeat the King of grace.

No spear shall pierce you,
No sea shall drown you,
No man shall wound you,
No woman lead you astray.

The cloak of Christ shall cover you,
The shadow of Christ be over you,
From the crown of your head
To the soles of your feet.

The sign of God is on you,
The name of God protects you,
Go forth in the name of the King,
In the strength of the Power.

You shall climb mountains,
Be not afraid.
God himself will guard your back,
Help you stand in battle fierce,
Stand against five hundred men,
And your enemies shall fall.

[*CG* 2.29]

Seun is here translated as 'sign' rather than the CG *version of 'charm'. The term is derived from the Old Irish* sén, *a benediction; though like many of the other prayers that invoke divine protection, this one is probably based on a much older pre-Christian incantation.*

The Anchorite's Prayer

Man or woman,
Dark or fair,
Whoever cursed you,
I will send
Power of the Father,
Power of the Son,
Power of the Spirit,
Three in One,
To thwart their evil will.

[*CG* 2.75]

This poem came from an old woman in Tiree who 'knew many such runes, but was forgetting them', according to Alexander Carmichael. An anchorite was a holy man or woman who lived alone, not in isolation like a hermit, but in a cell, possibly an enclosed cell, adjoining a church.

Fath Fith

Fath fith
Will I make on you,
By Mary's prophecy
And Brigid's veil.

From sheep, from ram,
From goat, from buck,
From fox, from wolf,
From sow, from boar,
From wild dog and cat,
From broad-hipped bear,
From cow, from horse,
From heifer, from bull,
From all the perils
Of hostile eyes
In forest and thicket,

From daughter, from son,
From birds of the air,
From the creeping things of earth,
From the fishes of the sea,
From the demons of the storm,
Fath fith.
Fith fath.

[*CG* 2.25]

'Fath fith' or 'Fith fath' (the terms are interchangeable) was an ancient incantation used by travellers, huntsmen or warriors, intended to render them invisible, and thus enable them to proceed without being seen by their enemies. In the teaching of the monks, this reminder of the many dangers to be encountered outside the crofts became a prayer for divine protection.

The Apostles' Charm

Peter and James and John
Glorious men, and true,
Come to your aid at the City's gate
In the presence of God the Son.

Against the sharp-eyed men,
Against the peering women,
Against the furies' arrows swift
And slender fairy darts.

Two people cursed you,
The Trinity shall save you.

Twenty-four diseases
Afflict both man and beast;
God search them, God scrape them, God cleanse them
From your blood and your flesh and your fragrant bones,
From this day forward, every day,
Till your time on earth is done.

[*CG* 2.59]

Fairy darts (seanga-sith) *was the term used for flint arrowheads; but in this
case, it may have had a more sinister meaning.*

Against Dangerous Women

Everlasting God of life,
Forgive me for my sins,
My wild thoughts and my foolish deeds,
My vulgar talk and false desires,
And all my shameful lusts.

Everlasting God of life,
Keep me safe from women,
From wanton women, silent women,
False women and spell-casting women,
And give me holy love.

No stain on my soul,
No stain on my body,
No taint on my breath,
O Father of all.

[*CG* 3.35]

*Because of their intimate association with the processes of birth and dying,
women were frequently suspected of using secret arts, spells and enchant-
ments derived from pagan religions. The male Islanders would have known
the story of Adam and Eve (Columba wrote a long poem on it) and the theme
of woman-as-temptress would have been a popular one.*

Against Invisible Enemies

Generous Chief of all the chiefs,
Bless me and mine for ever.
Bless me now in all I do
And hold me safe from harm,

From brownie and from banshee's threat,
From every nymph and water-wraith,
From every ogre on the hills,
From every monster pressing near,
From every ghost within the glen,
From every evil wish and grief,
Save me.

[*CG* 1.31]

In this rich collection of mythological evil forces, sith, *which recurs several times, is usually translated as 'fairy'; but Celtic fairies were not the delicate and winsome creatures of later fairy tales. They could be dangerous and destructive. The* sith *who accompanied the women at their looms had to be given bowls of milk or cream, otherwise it would spoil the cloth. A* gruagach *(brownie) might be induced to help in the house if placated, but was capable of much damage and mischief if offended. A* ban-sith *(banshee) was a female spirit which wailed, and warned of death in the house.* Glaistig *and* ban-nigh *refer to water-wraiths who lurked in the sea and in rivers, luring people to death by drowning.* Fruath *means a mountain ogre or troll, and may have been introduced during the Norwegian occupation of the Hebrides.*

Against Venom

Between me and every eye
May the eye of God be.

Between me and every purpose
May God's purpose be.

Between me and every hand
The hand of God be.

Between me and every pain
The pain of Christ be.

Between me and every love
The love of Christ be.

Between me and every wish
The wish of Christ be.

Between me and every will
The will of Christ be.

Between me and other powers
The power of Christ be.

There is no man can curse me,
No venom can wound me,
No ill thing can touch me.

[*CG* 3.57]

*A number of poems invoke the power of God against the evil eye, which it was
believed could kill or maim with a glance.*

Against the Four Enemies

An evil eye was on you,
A wicked mouth has cursed you,
An envious heart would harm you,
A crooked mind would eat you up.

These four are against you:
Man and wife,
Youth and maid.
Three come to protect you:
Father, Son,
And Spirit Holy.

Mary Mother succour you,
Bride the fair support you,
Columba kind come to your aid,
With saints and angel host.

If anyone has done you harm
With evil eye or evil wish,
May you be free of every ill,
And every form of malice.

In the name of God above,
Father, Son and Holy Ghost,
Round you now I weave this thread
To keep you safe from harm.

[CG 2.49]

*The last two lines suggest that this incantation involved a ritual of some kind,
probably carried out by a local wise woman.*

Peter and Paul, Save Us

Peter and Paul, save us,
Quiet Brigid, save us,
Holy Patrick, save us,

From the eye of little man,
From the eye of big man,
From the eye of the stranger
On the distant mountain.

From the eye of bird in sky,
From the eye of sea-bird fierce,
From the goose that passes by,
From the harsh and angry man,
From the hasty woman loud,
From the poisonous fangs of snakes.

Whole be he who blesses,
And whole be he who is blessed,
May we receive this blessing,
And you be whole this night.

[CG 4.181]

Exorcism

I will conquer the eye
As the duck conquers the lake,
As the swan conquers the river,
As the cow conquers the field,
And the hosts of God conquer all evil.

Power of wind I have over it,
Power of storm I have over it,
Power of fire I have over it,
Power of thunder I have over it,
Power of lightning I have over it,
Power of sun I have over it,
Power of moon I have over it,
Power of stars I have over it,
Power of the sky I have over it,
Power of the heavens and the distant worlds.

It shall be scattered
On the grey stones and the steep hills,
On the rushing falls and the meadows green,
Best of all, on the great salt sea
Which carries it away.

In the name of the Three of Life,
In the name of the Heavenly Three,
And of all the Secret Ones
And the Heavenly Powers.

[*CG* 2.45]

The belief that evil forces could be scattered by being sent to distant places also occurs in relation to pain and sickness: see Section 9.

Omens

All the signs were bad.

I heard the cuckoo with no food in my stomach,
I heard the stock-dove at the top of the tree,
I heard the sweet singer in the copse beyond,
And the night-owl screeching loud.

I saw the lamb hindquarters first,
I saw the foal with his rump to me,
I saw the snail on the bare flag-stone,
I saw the wheat all pitted with holes,
I saw the snipe while sitting bent,

And then I knew the year to come
Would not go well with me.

[*CG* 2.185]

It was considered bad luck to approach a horse or a sheep from the rear, or to see a foal or a lamb being born with its back to the viewer. The latter sight might have meant a breech birth. The wheat pitted with holes would be a sign of a poor harvest to come.

The Cockerel

Thus said the peasant women:
'The devil ruined me.
He lurks up there in the roof-beams,
And I cannot get him down.
Here you see in my cooking-pot
The quarters of a cock,
I cannot get the devil down
Till that cockerel crows again'.

The cockerel flew out of the pot
Up in the roof-beams high,
Folded his wings, and crowed aloud –
Sweet music to her ears.

God loves those who truly pray
With many a bitter tear,
He does not love a liar or cheat
Who takes his name in vain.

[*CG* 2.177]

Possibly a very old folk story, which occurs in several versions, has been given a Christian twist by the addition of the last verse. The devil was often suspected of lurking in the roof-beams, where his presence would be hidden by smoke from the peat fire.

A Comprehensive Curse

The charm of Mary, the charm of God
King of all the kings,
The strongest charm in all the world
Is mine to keep me safe.

Against small eye, against large eye,
Against the greedy women,
Against the hasty, greedy women,
The hasty and destructive women,

I make this powerful curse:
Against my eye,
Against your eye,
Against the eye of the grey man
Who came lately to my door.

She who caused you great distress
With envy, malice, jealousy,
May her lifeless body soon
Be floating on the loch.

May the eye lie in their eyes,
And on their sorceries,
May the eye take their jealousy,
Their malice, their ill-will.

May it lie on their cow calves,
And on their bull-calves,
May it lie on their heifers
And on their foaling mares.

May it lie on their small children
And on their children grown,
May it lie on their bleating goats,
And on their woolly sheep.

May it lie on their potent men,
On women bearing child,
Their sons unable sons to bear,
Their daughters barren stock.

May the eye affect their spinal cords,
And strain their sinews taut,
Whatever things they value most,
The evil eye destroy.

So may they groan and suffer grief,
And yawn with misery,
May tears of sadness fill their eyes
And loud be their lament.

Send them to the prey-birds,
Send them to the beasts,
Send them to the tree-tops,
And to the withered heath.
Send them to the mountain-tops,
Send them to the sea.

One third today,
Two thirds tomorrow
All thirds till doomsday
The day after.

[*CG* 4.159]

The fear of women comes through quite strongly in this poem – particularly of women who are swift and determined in their actions, and loud or strident in speech. Women were expected to be peaceful and submissive, and to be quiet when the men spoke. There is also evidence of the common fear of the stranger, who represented the unknown, and whose intentions were possibly hostile. The tone in this poem is that of the comminatory Psalms rather than that of the Gospels. The enemies were to be scattered in a thoroughly Old Testament fashion.

8
herbs and plants

The Wild Violet

I will pick the violet,
Gentle flower of peace,
In the name of God the King
Son, and Spirit holy,
In the name of Mary pure,
Of Michael and of Bride.

In the heat of battle,
Blood and pain and death,
I call upon you, blessed plant.
Bring me solace, bring me joy,
Under the shield of God.

[*CG* 2.111]

The mothan, *a bog-violet or thyme-leaved sandwort, was much prized as a token of long life and good fortune. It was used as a love-charm, carried by travellers and by warriors in battle, and placed under pillows to ensure a safe delivery for women in labour.*

The Shamrock

Four leaves on a straight root,
A straight stem from the root,
Promising us the seven joys
Without a trace of ill.

Joy of health,
Joy of friends,
Joy of cattle,
Joy of sheep,
Joy of sons and daughters fair,
Joy of peace,
And joy of God.

[*CG* 2.107]

The shamrock was a symbol of the Trinity because it consisted of three leaves bound by a common stalk, and St Patrick is reputed to have used it as a teaching aid. It does not figure prominently in CG, as it does in Irish writing of the period. By the time Dr Carmichael made his collection of poems some 14 centuries later, Scotland had its own proud traditions, and the Western Isles were politically part of Scotland, and not of Ireland. It is not clear whether the shamrock was never prominent in the traditions of the Isles, or whether it was gradually more or less abandoned in the Scottish interest.

Saint John's Wort

Saint John's Wort, Saint John's Wort,
Fortunate is he
Who plucks you with his right hand,
Preserves you with his left hand.
If he finds you in the cattle fold,
Many shall be his kine.

I will keep my little plant
As a prayer to my King,
To quiet the wrath of men of blood,
And stay the wiles of women.

I will keep my little plant
As a prayer to my King,
To give me strength and keep me safe
In all I say or do.

I will keep my little plant
As a prayer to the Three,
Father, Son and Spirit,
And Mary, mother mild.

[CG 2.97]

St John's Wort, now sold by many herbalists and medically recognized as a cure for mild or medium depression, was greatly prized as a herb. It was thought to be efficacious only if found accidentally rather than deliberately sought for.

Columba's Plant

Little plant of Columba,
Found without seeking,
Stay under my arm for ever.

For friendship,
For prosperity,
For all I hope to achieve:

Good fortune with sheep, with goats, with fowl,
Good fortune in fields, and with fish in the stream,
In growing food and breeding cows,
With my friends, and with my young,
In battle, that I win my cause,
On land and sea, on oceans wide,
Through the Trinity above,
Through the Three who hold me close,
Through the great eternal Three,
Little plant, protect me.

[*CG* 2.101]

St John's Wort was known as Allas Chaluim-Chille, *the glory of St Columba. The saint is said to have carried the plant under his arm as a sign of reverence for St John the Baptist, and many people followed this custom of wearing an 'armpit package' in the hope of good fortune and protection.*

Myrtle

Gracious red myrtle,
Kindly bog-myrtle,
In the name of the Trinity
Let me pick your flowers.

In the name of the Father,
Son and Spirit eternal,
The source of all virtues,
Let me live a good life.

For virtue in men,
And virtue in women,
For virtue in loving
And a long, healthy span,

For virtue in ventures,
And virtue in prospects,
For a life without peril,
Unstained by reproach.

[CG 4.137]

The Passion Flower

There is no land, no ocean,
No lake, no mountain height,
No forest deep, that is not safe
When I have the passion flower.

Passion flower of virtues,
Made holy by the Lamb,
Son of Mother Mary,
Symbol of his blood.

[CG 2.115]

The passion flower (passiflora aceae) is a climbing plant still grown in many gardens. It was widely held to be symbolic of Christ's crucifixion because of its markings: the leaves symbolize the spear that pierced his side, the five anthems (parts of the stamens containing pollen) the five wounds, the tendrils the whips, the central column the pillar of the cross, the threads within the flowers the crown of thorns, and the calyx the glory of his sacrifice.

The Pearlwort

I will pick the pearlwort
Under the sun on Sunday
Under the hand of the Virgin,
Who willed it to grow.

While I keep the pearlwort,
My mouth shall speak no harm,
My eye shall see no ill,
My hand shall hurt nothing,
My heart shall be light,
And my death shall be easy.

[*CG* 4.135]

The pearlwort was a rare plant found in moorland and on hills. It had red roots, and five- or six-pointed leaves. Christian legends were associated with it: that it was the plant on which Christ first placed his foot when he came to earth, or after the Resurrection, or that he lay on it when away from his enemies. A bunch of pearlwort over the lintel was held to prevent the sluagh *or 'airy host' from entering the house. It was also used as a love-philtre, to help women in labour, to thwart evildoers, and to cure sick cows.*

Silverweed

Honey under ground,
Silverweed in the spring,
In summer, sweet as seasoning
Whisked into the whey.

Sweet and fruity silverweed
Like carrots in the autumn,
Sweet and crispy silverweed
Like nuts in the winter,
Between the Feast of Andrew
And Holy Christmastide.

[*CG* 4.119]

Silverweed was a root vegetable cultivated and much used before the intro-duction of the potato in the seventeenth century. It could be boiled or roasted, or ground into meal for bread or porridge. It could evidently be harvested almost all the year round, and was considered both nutritious and tasty. St Andrew's Day is 30 November, so the winter season was evidently a short one.

The Yarrow

When I pick the yarrow
My look shall be more kindly,
My lips more warm,
My speech more modest,
My lips as sweet as strawberry juice.

May I be an island at sea,
A hill on the shore,
A star in the sky
When the old moon is waning,
A staff to the weak.

I will be strong against any man,
And none can harm me.

[CG 2.95]

The yarrow (millefolium) *is a perennial herb still used for snuff and herb tea. According to the Saxon text* Leechdoms, Wort-cunning and Starcraft, *the Saxons thought it a sovereign cure for toothache, wounds, swellings, bladder trouble and ache of the guts, but the Islanders appear to have taken a more poetic view of its uses.*

The Aspen

Curses on you, aspen tree!
On you was crucified
The fair young King of all the world,
Nailed to the Cross,
Nailed to the Cross,
The Cross on which he died.

Curses on you, aspen cruel!
On you was crucified
The sinless King of glory bright,
In bitter pain,
In bitter pain,
His blood in streams outpoured.

Curses on you, aspen doomed!
On you was crucified
The King of kings, the Lord of Truth.
Who curse you not,
Who curse you not,
May they be cursèd too.

[*CG* 2.105]

The aspen, a species of poplar with fluttering leaves, is sometimes called 'the shiver tree'. It was thought to have been the wood of Christ's cross, condemned after the crucifixion to quiver in guilt in the stillest air.

The Reed

Reed unholy,
Reed unblest,
Reed which bore
The cursèd drink!

Every wind that howls
Over hill and plain
Carries the death-groan
Of the dying Christ.

[*CG* 4.127]

After Christ had called his great cry of desolation from the Cross, Eloi, Eloi, lama sabachthani, *one of the watchers soaked a sponge in sour wine, and put it on a stick, so that he could drink and dull his pain (Matt. 27.53; Mark 15.61). This stick was thought to be a reed, though St John's Gospel (19.29) says that it was a branch of hyssop. The reed was also looked on as accursed because the soldiers who mocked Christ before the crucifixion put a reed in his hand to symbolize the authority of a sceptre when he was hailed as 'King of the Jews' (Matt. 27.29). There are also Old Testament references to 'bruised reeds' and 'shaken reeds'.*

Seaweed

Come from the sea is seaweed,
Red and yellow seaweed,
Tangles thrown upon the shore
Left by the ebbing tide.

Gentle Brigid, Mary mild,
Patrick, saint of power,
Michael, bring us seaweed,
To fertilise our land.

[*CG* 4.33]

The women probably gathered seaweed, which was used for several different purposes. It was the only ready source of salt, which was essential for preserving meat, game or fish. Lumps of salt, highly prized, were sometimes brought by ship; but it could also be extracted from seaweed by a process of burning the weed and boiling the ash. Seaweed was widely used, as this poem suggests, as fertilizer on the soil, which was mostly poor. One kind of seaweed washed up on the shores by the prevailing westerly winds is edible, and known as carragheen. In a long period of calm, the people would 'hope and pray for the coming of seaweed', being anxious at the prospect of a poor harvest.

9
ḥealíɳg

Against Diseases

The rune of the holy maiden Bride
For the crippled seaman,
For crooked limb, for broken bones,
For the nine painful diseases
And the three poisonous diseases,
Deny it not to women,
Deny it not to beasts.

Christ went on a horse,
The horse broke its leg,
Christ went down,
And made the leg whole.

As Christ made whole that,
May Christ make whole this,
And may he do more,
If it so be his will.

Columba made a prayer
At the foot of the glen,
For bleeding vein, for painful joint.
Now you are sick,
Tomorrow be whole.

[CG 2.15]

The story of Christ healing the lame horse occurs in a number of Irish legends of the period, though there is no biblical foundation for it.

For a Sick Girl

Christ told Simon Peter
To feed his people,
To teach his people,
To shield his people,
To aid his people,
To save his people
From loss and betrayal.

Dear God,
The King of all good,
Take now the wasting,
The weakness and weariness,
Seizures and ailments,
Soreness and malady,
Sickness and pain
This maiden suffers.

Send them to the distant beasts,
That prowl on the mountains,
Send them to the wild ones
That crawl on deserts far,
Send them to the winged ones
That fly above the summits,
Send them to the monsters of the brine.

Send them to the flowing streams,
Send them to the hill-bogs,
Send them to the whales
And to the wheeling birds.

May the God of guidance scatter
The ills that plague my sister.
They will not harm the birds and beasts,
And my sister will be well.

[*CG* 4.259]

Illnesses, like evil intentions, were regarded as malignant entities that could be separated from the sufferer and sent elsewhere: compare the story of the Gadarene swine (Matt. 8.28–32; Mark 5.11–13; Luke 8.32–3).

Heart Pains

Arrows fasten on my heart
With agonising pain,
And in my fear, I call upon
Patrick, kindly saint,
To cure me now as once he cured
The mother of a king.

Twenty-four diseases
Are found in man and beast,
In strong men, and in women,
In their sons and daughters fair.

I call upon Saint Patrick,
By the rushing stream,
By the standing stones of earth,
To heal my heart today.

[*CG* 4.267]

The 'chest disease' sounds like angina. The prayer, which is incomplete, goes on to list a number of other diseases, including smallpox, jaundice, ague, whooping cough, fever, the wasting disease, the throat disease, the neck disease and measles.

A Chest Seizure

(This invocation is addressed to the pain.)

Power of sun and power of moon,
Power of rain and power of dew,
Power of land and power of sea,
Power of stars and power of sky,
Power of saints and power of God,
All these I have over you.

Go to the grey stones,
Go to the mountains,
Go to the waterfalls,
Go to the clouds,
Go to the ocean whales,
Go to the swamps and moors,
Go to the sea-waves.
The great surging ocean
Shall sweep you away.

The saints shall uphold me,
Soothing me gently,
In the power of the Trinity
Who gives us life.

[CG 4.257]

Gall-stones

I have a charm for gravel,
The red disease, the dread disease,
That irritates the bladder
And causes bleeding sore.

As the river runs cold,
As the mill grinds fast,
Stop the bleeding,
Make the water flow.

In the name of the Father,
In the name of the Son,
In the name of the Spirit,
God Three in One.

[*CG* 2.125]

Gall-stones in the bladder or bile duct cause inflammation and bleeding, with painful blockages in the urinary tract.

Sprains and Strains

Christ, who rode so calmly
Upon a donkey's back,
Healed the sore and bloody wounds,
Cheered the sad and outcast,
Gave the weary rest.

Christ set free the prisoner,
Old and young he freed,
Healed the blind, the deaf, the lame,
Raised Lazarus from the dead.

Christ gave strength to Peter,
Christ gave strength to Paul,
Strength he gave to the Mother of tears,
And Brigid of the flock.

Soothing and salving,
With Columba's plant,
I invoke the God of life,
I invoke the Christ of love,
And the Spirit's grace.

[*CG* 4.209]

The 'Mother of tears' is the Blessed Virgin Mary, with whom St Brigid is again associated. Columba's plant, St John's Wort, was evidently rubbed on the affected limb.

Rupture

God of grace,
Make whole my body,
Christ of the Passion,
Restore my soul,
Spirit of wisdom,
Give me tranquillity,
That I may sleep in peace.

Father of all life,
Give me strength in my weakness,
Jesus the loving,
Take now the pain,
Spirit most holy,
Reduce this sore rupture,
That I may sleep in peace.

[*CG* 4.279]

A hernia, or rupture of the body cavities, usually the abdomen or diaphragm, is both painful and disabling. In a society where men's status depended on their ability to lift heavy weights or to pull a boat ashore, and where there were no surgical techniques, it would have been a devastating affliction.

Toothache

The worm in my head is torturing me,
The pain in my head is agony,
The teeth of hell are gnawing at me,
Bride, cure my hellish teeth.

Lovely Bride, now succour me,
Mary's power encompass me,
Through my life, pray let it be
That my teeth stay in my head.

[*CG* 2.11]

It was widely believed that toothache was caused by a worm. There were special toothache wells, where sufferers would go to find relief from what must have been a very common ailment. Natural teeth were very important when there was no alternative, and the diet consisted largely of meat, which had to be chewed. Those without teeth would have been reduced to eating pap or gruel.

10
ᴅay By ᴅay

Walking with God

With God be my walking this day,
With Christ be my walking this day,
With Spirit be my walking this day,
The Three-fold all-kindly my way,
Ho! Ho! Ho! the Three-fold all-kindly I pray.

God the Father shield me,
God the Son shield me,
God the Spirit shield me,
As Three and as One.

Shield me this day from evil,
Shield me this night from harm.
Ho! Ho! my soul and my body,
Keep them safe today.

[*CG* 3.49]

The first verse of this poem, in metrical form, is well known, since it has appeared in a number of Celtic anthologies. This version is taken from David Adam's The Cry of the Deer: Meditations on the Hymn of St Patrick *(SPCK, 1987), p. 145.*

Morning Prayer

God, who brought me through the night
Of rest and darkness, to the light
Of joyous day, now stay with me,
So that my final rest shall be
In joy and light eternally.

[CG 1.33]

*Through the many hours of winter darkness, people whose only light came
from a peat fire or a home-made tallow candle would have looked for the
dawn, and seen in it a promise of the light of heaven.*

I Come This Day

I come this day to the Father,
I come this day to the Son,
To the Holy Spirit, powerful,
To God, the Three in One.

Father, Spirit and Jesus,
Be with me, I pray,
From the crown of my head to the soles of my feet,
Watch over me this day.

All that I am I offer,
Everything I own,
Shelter me, Lord Jesus,
Leave me not alone.

[CG 1.69]

The Branch of Glory

O God,
In my deeds,
In my speech,
In my reason,
And in the granting of my desires,
In my sleep,
In my dreams,
In my rest,
In my thoughts,
In my heart and soul,
May the blessed Virgin Mary
And the promised Branch of Glory dwell.

In my heart always,
May the blessed Virgin Mary
And the fragrant Branch of Glory dwell.

[*CG* 1.27]

In older versions of the Old Testament, including the Authorized and Revised Versions, Isaiah 4.2 reads, 'In that day, shall the branch of the Lord be beautiful and glorious'. 'The branch of the Lord' is changed in the New English Bible to 'the plant that the Lord has grown'; but there are many other Old Testament references to the promised Messiah as a branch, e.g. 'a righteous branch of David' (Jer. 33.15), 'my Servant, the Branch' (Zech. 3.8), and 'the man whose name is The Branch' (Zech. 6.12), so this expression would have been familiar in the Celtic Church.

Consecrate Us

Jesu, Son of Mary,
Have mercy on us.
Jesu, Son of Mary,
Grant us your peace.

Be with us when life dawns,
And at the darkening of life's day.

Consecrate us,
High or low,
Rich or poor,
In good and ill fortune,
Heart and body,
Day by day,
Night by night,
Thou King of kings,
Thou God of all.

[CG 1.19]

God, Give Me Wisdom

God, give me wisdom,
God, give me strength,
Correct me with justice
And mercy at last.

God, give me plenty
And shield me from harm.
God, give me grace
Through the merits of Christ,

Christ, seed of David,
Who preached in the Temple,
Sacrificed in the Garden,
Who died for me.

[CG 1.65]

The reference in the penultimate line is to Christ's submission to the will of God in Gethsemane, 'My Father, if it is possible, let this cup pass from me: yet not what I want but what you want' (Matt. 26.39; Mark 14.36; Luke 22.42), rather than to his subsequent crucifixion, which took place across the Kedron Valley outside the walls of Jerusalem.

Shepherd of the Flock

You are the Shepherd of the flock,
Keep safe our house and fold,
Shield and Protector, keep us safe,
And guard us evermore.

Be our Shield, and hold us firm
Against the powers of hell,
Against the fiends that seek our souls,
In the foul smoke of the abyss.

May my soul trust God alone,
King of kings and Lord of lords,
May Saint Michael, saint of power,
Take it safe to heaven.

[CG 1.37]

References in the second verse to fiends and the abyss suggest Jewish apocalyptic sources.

God in All Things

God to enfold me,
God to surround me,
God in my speaking,
God in my thinking,

God in my sleeping,
God in my waking,
God in my watching,
God in my hoping,

God in my life,
God on my lips,
God in my soul,
God in my heart,

God in my day's work,
God in my slumber,
God in my living soul,
Here and in heaven.

[*CG* 3.53]

I Kneel and Pray

I kneel and pray
To the Father who made me,
To the Son who died for me,
To the Spirit who cleansed me:

Save us from disaster,
Grant us your love –
  the affection of God,
  the smile of God,
  the wisdom of God,
  the grace of God,
  the majesty of God.

In this world of the Three,
Grant us the will
To serve you below
As the saints do in heaven.

Each shade and light,
Each day and night,
Grant us your peace.

[CG 1.3]

Preserve Me Tonight

Jesus without sin,
Who suffered great pain,
When wicked men hung you
To die on the Cross,

Save me from evil,
Save me from harm,
Save my frail body,
And bless me tonight.

Give me your strength,
Great Herdsman of might,
Do not forsake me,
Preserve me tonight.

[*CG* 1.71]

Bed Blessing

I am lying down, as I should
In the fellowship of Christ,
In the fellowship of the Father
And the Spirit of great power.

I am lying down with God,
And God shall lie down with me,
I will not lie down with sin,
Nor sin's shadow lie with me.

[*CG* 1.83]

11
soul journey

To a Guardian Angel

On the sea of unrighteousness,
My frail coracle sails
Through narrows and straits
Of temptation and threat.

God sent you to guard me,
To keep me from harm,
Be a bright flame before me,
A bright star to lead me,
A smooth path to follow,
A shepherd behind me
Tonight and for ever.

I am tired, and a stranger,
I want to go home
To the land of the angels,
And heaven's own peace.

[*CG* 1.49]

Sinners All

God, the all-powerful
Father of love,
Thanks be to you, Lord,
For the blessings of life.

Whatever befalls us
In fortune or lot
Comes with your rich gifts,
Given with joy.

We are all sinners,
Guilty and weak,
Stained with wrong-doing
In mind, heart and flesh,
Wrong thoughts and wrong actions.
Our sins pile up high.
Leap over them, good Lord,
With love's healing power.

In the path of our calling,
Through sunlight and dark,
Through comfort and suffering,
Guide us in your way.

Shield us and guard us
Throughout life's span,
That we may sing in glory
Where no tears are shed.

[*CG* 1.23]

In the last verse, Alexander Carmichael has 'Be about the beginning and end of our race'; the translation of the Gaelic reis is 'race', but the reference here is clearly to the span of an individual human life, not to racial continuity.

God, Listen to Me

God, listen to me,
Bend down your ear,
Let my supplications
Rise and be heard.

Come down, King of Glory,
To save and protect me.
Son of the Virgin,
Surround me with power.

[CG 1.13]

This prayer was probably inspired by Psalm 31: 'In thee, O Lord, have I put my trust . . . bow down thine ear to me: make haste to deliver me' (AV).

Repentance

God be with us
On this his day,
God be with us,
On this his night.

Since we came into the world,
We have deserved his wrath.
Grant us forgiveness,
Merciful Lord.

If we have done evil,
If any accuse us,
Make it plain to us,
Root it from our hearts.

Banish it from us,
That we may be fit to stay
Where we shall longest be,
In your presence for ever.

[CG 1.15]

Youth and Age

Now you are healthy,
You hold your head high,
And you scorn to offer
Devotion to God.

Now you are haughty,
Greedy and proud,
Careless in speaking,
Never ashamed.

But when it is winter
In pain and distress,
You'll shake your head sadly
And bow it to earth.

No longer handsome,
No longer strong,
You'll come as a beggar
On your two knees.

[CG 2.187]

Growing Old

The cruel mob turned against you,
And hanged you on a tree.
Now that I am old and grey,
Lord Jesus, pity me.

When I was young, I broke your laws,
In age, I am dejected,
Filled with guilt and steeped in sin,
One cymbal, now rejected.

Before the Son of God came down
The earth was black with storm,
No stars, no sun, no moon, no light,
No beating heart, no form.

But when the Son of God came,
He shone on the great green sea,
He lit up all the hills and plains,
In glorious majesty.

[*CG* 2.173]

An clab-goileam bochd bua'all – '*a poor clattering cymbal*' *the imagery of the single cymbal suggests that the singer is an old man or woman mourning the death of a marriage partner.*

The City of God

Jesus without sin,
King of the poor,
Sorely oppressed
By wicked men,

Great King of Heaven,
Succour my soul,
Which you bought at the cost
Of your own sacred life.

For the sake of your Passion,
In this time of my sorrow,
Take me in safety
To the City of God.

[*CG*1.77]

Peace to the Weary

I am weary, weak and cold,
Weary of crossing land and sea,
Weary of stumbling over the moor,
Weary of wave, and weary of trough.
Grant me your peace.

Help all who travail on land or sea,
Help them through grief and bitter tears,
Still their distress, and heal their wounds,
Grant them your peace this night.

Beloved Father of us all,
Accept my grief, my tears,
Through the merits of your Son
Jesus, who died for me.

Lead me to the house of peace,
Lead me to rest with him
In his gentle haven
Of mercy at the last.

[*CG*2.177]

New Moon

New moon of the heavens,
How many of us have gone
Across the black abyss of death
Since the last time you shone?

So many men and women
Have crossed, yet even so
God's mercy still allows me
To praise him here below.

[*CG* 3.289]

The End and the Beginning

When the soul leaves the body,
The stubborn body,
And goes, in bursts of light
Up from out its human frame,
In its final flight,

God, come and find me,
Come to seek and find me,
God and Jesus, Mary's Son,
Virgin and Apostles twelve,
Seek me and find me
When my life is done.

[*CG* 3.395]

Part 3

collecting and editing
carmina gadelica

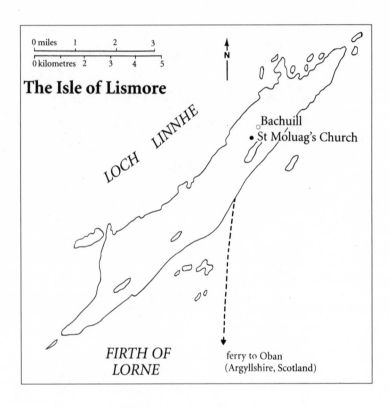

0 miles   1   2   3
0 kilometres   2   3   4   5

N

The Isle of Lismore

LOCH LINNHE

Bachuill
• St Moluag's Church

FIRTH OF
LORNE

ferry to Oban
(Argyllshire, Scotland)

Alexander Carmichael.

collecting and editing
carmina gadelica

Alexander Carmichael was an Islander himself, but only by a short distance. He came from the island of Lismore, which is to the north of Oban in Scotland, in the Firth of Lorne. Today the ferry journey takes about half an hour. Lismore, which is about six miles long and a mile wide, is sparsely populated. The Carmichael family held land there, and claimed connections with the church established by St Moluag, a missionary monk from either Benn Chorr or Iona, in the late sixth century.[1] The church is still standing, and St Moluag's blackthorn staff (*Bachuill* in Gaelic) is preserved as a precious heritage from 'the age of the saints'.[2]

Alexander was born on 1 December, 1832. He went to the Greenock Academy, and then to a collegiate school (a type of grammar school) in Edinburgh. He wanted to make a career in the army, and the Duke of Argyll promised him a commission in his own regiment; but for an army commission in a good regiment he needed a private income. When his father died, there was no money to make this possible. Alexander had to earn his living, and his uncle, a minister in the Church of Scotland, helped him to obtain a nomination for the Civil Service. He became a clerk in the Inland Revenue Service.[3]

After being based at Greenock, Dublin and Cornwall in his early career, he was posted to positions in the Western Isles, based in Skye, Barra and South Uist. He became an expert on land taxation, and a developed a great sympathy for the crofters, who were being evicted from their land by unscrupulous landlords. He provided written evidence for the Royal Commission on Crofting of 1885, which led to the Crofters (Holdings) Act of 1886.[4] This Act protected poor crofters and their families, establishing a Land Court to set fair rents and prevent rack-renting.

Alexander Carmichael's travels took him to many parts of the Isles. He became fascinated by the religious songs of the Islanders, which he saw as 'the product of faraway thinking, come down on the long stream of time . . . from the cloistered cells of Derry and Iona'. He wrote down for the first time 'words worn and polished by the sea of music'. Some were sung, some intoned, and some 'recited in a curiously rhythmic monotone'.[5] He travelled the Isles on foot, tramping sheeptracks and bridle paths, and often spending nights in the open when there was no shelter nearby. He crossed from island to island by ford and ferry, sometimes in dangerous conditions. He wrote in his Introduction to *Carmina Gadelica* of the passages between the islands of the Outer Hebrides, 'The Atlantic rushes through these straits and narrows into the Minch, and the Minch rushes through the straits and narrows into the Atlantic, four times every twenty-four hours. The constant rushing to and fro of these mighty waters is very striking.'[6] His successor was drowned negotiating one of the passages.[7]

He had an intense love of the Isles and their people. Though his own means were limited, he helped many poor crofting families with gifts of food, and even paid their land tax himself on occasions. Though he was offered promotion to a post in the Inland Revenue office in Edinburgh, he refused to leave the Isles for many years. He married at the age of 38, and it was not until his children were growing up and needed good schools that he finally agreed to the move.[8]

While he was still travelling in the Isles, he became a corresponding member of the Society of Antiquaries of Scotland, and wrote for the *Celtic Review*. When he and his family moved to Edinburgh, he began to sift and collate the material he had collected from the crofters, and to prepare some of it for publication in book form.

In March 1898 he wrote to Fr Allan McDonald, a Roman Catholic parish priest on Eriskay, South Uist:

> I had another secret hope in my soul – that by making the book up in as good a form as I could in matter and material, it might perhaps be the means of conciliating some future politician in favour of our dear Highland people. For example, had the book been in the hands of Mr Gladstone some twenty years ago, who knows but it might have interested him still more in our dear lovable people.[9]

He wanted to 'show the world that our dearly beloved people were not the rude, barbarous, creedless, godless, ignorant men and women that prejudiced writers have represented them'.[10]

Working on *Carmina Gadelica*

When Alexander Carmichael settled in Edinburgh after leaving the Isles, the preparation of the Songs became a family industry. He had brought back a mass of jottings in Gaelic. Where did he write them? In dimly lit farm cottages, in stables, on bleak hillsides, sitting on the shore? On what? The pages of notebooks, odd sheets of paper, the backs of envelopes? His work meant travelling on foot over rough country, and carrying his own baggage.

The task of transcribing and presenting this material was a huge one. In his Introduction, he pays tribute to his wife for her 'unfailing sympathy and cultured ear', and thanks her for copying from ancient Celtic manuscripts the Celtic letters that ornament his text, work that required 'great skill and patient care owing to the defaced condition of the originals'. Of course there were no photocopying facilities at the time, and it seems that even photography was not sufficiently advanced to make mechanical copies possible. His three sons 'helped in various ways', and his daughter Elizabeth (Ella) seems to have been almost a full-time assistant: she transcribed documents, corrected proofs (which must have been a very lengthy and exacting task) and 'acted as amanuensis throughout'.[11]

He felt that the work was difficult, but urgent:

> With each succeeding generation, Gaelic speech becomes more limited and Gaelic phraseology more obscure. Both reciter and writer felt this when words and phrases occurred which neither knew. I can only hope that in the near or distant future, some competent scholar may compare these gleanings of mine with Celtic writings at home and abroad, and that light may be shed upon what is to me obscure.[12]

At this time, no Scottish university had a department of Celtic or Gaelic Studies, and academic assistance was hard to come by, though he does thank 'Mr George Henderson, M.A. Edin., Ph.D. Leipzig, B. Litt. Oxon.' for unspecified help and sustained encouragement. According to the antiquarian laird of Canna, John Lorne Campbell, Dr Henderson had already published three books of his own, including one for the Irish Texts Society. He 'saved Carmichael from some bad solecisms', and added most of the learned references in Volume 2. Campbell comments, 'The addition of such learned references (Henderson as source unmentioned) to Carmichael's notes, which otherwise contain a good many unreferenced historical, literary and linguistic assertions, produces rather a peculiar combination.'[13]

Alexander Carmichael was very conscious of his own lack of formal education, and regretted that he was not 'better qualified to treat what I have collected'. There were times when he despaired, 'painfully conscious' of his own failures. He translated very literally, word for word, afraid to move away from Gaelic grammar and Gaelic word order. Gaelic, unlike English and most European languages, does not have a present tense. Instead, it uses the verbal noun or gerund. It is not possible to say 'I pray' but only 'I am praying' – hence such odd-sounding phrases as 'I am bending my knee' or 'With God be my walking this day'. Also, Gaelic speakers often use the historic present: the result should not surprise anyone who has heard an Irishman say something like, 'Now here am I coming down the street, and I'm meeting Kelly, and we're talking about O'Shaughnessy.' Such constructions make for vivid story-telling, but they can be something of a hindrance in translation, particularly in poetry.

Perhaps not many people study the main volumes of *Carmina Gadelica* these days. Even the title is off-putting. The volumes are large and heavy, only to be found in academic libraries, and exceedingly wordy. Often the same song is given in several different versions picked up on different islands, and they are not easy reading. Sometimes alternative translations are offered. Some of the poems are incomplete, and some – probably where two different versions have been elided – are long and repetitious; but Alexander Carmichael was trying to satisfy the Gaelic specialists, and to save what he thought was a dying language. He writes in his Introduction, 'Again and again I laid down my self-imposed task, feeling unable to render the intense power and supreme beauty of the original Gaelic into adequate English.'[14]

Publication of Volumes 1 and 2

A benefactor offered to pay for the publication of the book. This offer, though appreciated, was refused. Alexander Carmichael, by this time a retired civil servant with a small pension, cannot have been a rich man, but the book was his, and he paid for publication himself. He finally published two volumes in 1900 under the sonorous title of *Carmina Gadelica*, in a limited edition, 'sumptuously bound', to express his high esteem for 'the folk whose ways and thoughts the volumes enshrine'.[15] In his later years, when the value of his work in interpreting the traditions of the Columban Church and the way of life of the people of the Western Isles was widely acclaimed in Scottish academic circles, he became an honorary Doctor of Law in the University of Edinburgh, and Honorary President of the Celtic Societies of Edinburgh, Glasgow and St Andrews.[16]

Alexander Carmichael died on St Columba's Day, 9 June 1912 in his eightieth year, and was buried in the churchyard of St Moluag's Church on Lismore, but the family's work went on in his memory. His daughter, by that time Elizabeth Carmichael Watson, wife of a professor in the University of Edinburgh, republished his two volumes in 1928 in a more accessible edition, with only minor typographical corrections.[17]

Volumes 3 and 4

Some 20 years after that, Elizabeth's son, James Carmichael Watson, became Professor of Celtic Studies in the University of Edinburgh, and took on the task of publishing further volumes from the mass of papers that the Collector had bequeathed to his family.

Professor Watson was a trained Gaelic scholar, which his grandfather was not; but he did not have Alexander Carmichael's knowledge of the Isles and the Islanders and his first-hand acquaintance with the oral traditions. It must have been a very difficult undertaking. He clearly did not wish to present an academic work that might implicitly be held to criticize his grandfather's labours. The new volumes had to be congruent with the published ones, and he determined to add nothing of his own. So he used his grandfather's translations, even when his own academic experience suggested a different rendering. He wrote, 'I have done so deliberately, thinking that to know what these passages meant to their reciters and Collector (who had a knowledge of Gaelic more intimate than anyone can claim now) is not less valuable than to know what they meant to their ancestors centuries before.'[18] From an academic point of view he was dealing with very unsatisfactory material. The originals were scattered and disconnected, and he complained of 'various people having transcribed my grandfather's not always legible hand',[19] but he felt impelled to do his best with it. There may have been pressure from the surviving Carmichaels, though his mother had died by this time. There would certainly have been pressure from Scottish literary circles, in which *Carmina Gadelica* was held in high esteem, and possibly from the authorities of the University of Edinburgh, who had appointed him Professor of Celtic Studies while still in his late twenties. His Carmichael blood, his University of Edinburgh connections and his possession of the Carmichael papers may have been key factors in his appointment.

John Lorne Campbell describes how Professor Watson began his work on the papers in 1939. He was writing under considerable pressure. In October 1939 he wrote, 'I am wondering whether I'll ever get the 2 vols. of *Carmina* out, and if I don't what will happen to them . . . There are other things I'd like published, but that is far the most important.' In November 1939 he wrote that he had begun work on Volumes 3 and 4, 'thinking that if I don't do it now, I may never'. World War Two had broken out, and he was already pressing the authorities to allow him to join the Royal Navy.

He must have worked at top speed, and completed the third volume in a matter of months. It amounted to nearly 400 pages of text, and was published before the end of 1940. Volume 4, nearly as long, followed in 1941.[20] In August of that year, James Carmichael Watson finally enlisted in the Royal Navy, and nine months later he was killed on active service. He was 32 years old.

Volume 5

After the war, a fifth volume was edited by Angus Matheson, Senior Lecturer in Celtic Studies in the University of Glasgow;[21] but this volume is almost entirely devoted to minor folklore, poems about charms and fairies, and is not of the same quality as the earlier volumes. From his bundle of material, much of it transcribed by other people, Alexander Carmichael had selected the best for his two volumes. Professor Watson took the best of what remained; and there was not much left for Volume 5. The quality declines with each volume, as there is less and less found worth reproducing out of an increasingly limited pool of material. The poems in Volumes 1 and 2, the Collector's own favourites, are, not surprisingly, the ones most often read and quoted.

Part 4
critics and contexts

CRÍTICS and contexts

The poems and prayers in *Carmina Gadelica* clearly reflect the teaching of the Celtic monks many centuries before. They must have been modified over the centuries – but not unrecognizably. Metre and rhyme help to keep a poem in its original form. Most of us can recite 'Ride a cock horse to Banbury Cross' without stopping to reflect on the fate of the thirteenth century Queen Eleanor of Castile whose funeral cortège it commemorates. People with a single language and no written records develop very strong oral traditions, and often have excellent memories, exercised by repetition.

The savage attacks from Danish invaders in the ninth century led to the decline of the eastern seaways and the islands became remote from outside influence. Churches and monasteries were sacked, ships no longer came from the Mediterranean, and Ireland and Scotland developed their own national concerns. The surviving crofters, marginalized and largely left to their own devices, kept to their traditional ways and their traditional speech.

Alexander Carmichael's careful recordings, which he described as 'like the fragments of a Greek or Etruscan vase',[1] caused him much trouble in editing, because he was painfully aware of the limitations of his own academic background. They caused his grandson even more trouble, because he was committed to editing Volumes 3 and 4 in a very different context – that of a Celtic scholar who was the head of a Department of Celtic Studies in a prestigious university. The task had to be undertaken, but he must have been very much aware that his own academic reputation was at stake.

· *Carmina Gadelica* became part of Scots literary history, much lauded by Scots writers, but not widely studied outside Scotland. It was not until the late 1970s, in a period when revisionism became the fashion, that Carmichael's considerable reputation was seriously attacked by people working in quite different contexts. Even so, the argument remained largely confined to specialist Gaelic journals until 1999, when Dr Ian Bradley, a popular writer on Celtic spirituality, published a new paperback.

Celtic Christianity

Dr Bradley, Senior Lecturer in Practical Theology in the University of St Andrews, and a Presbyterian minister, is the author of *The Celtic Way*, first published in 1993, which has enjoyed considerable success and run to repeated reprints. In the Introduction to *Celtic Christianity*, published six years later, he makes it clear that he thinks that the popularity of the movement has got out of hand. The subject 'attracts New Agers, post-modernists, liberals, feminists, environmentalists, evangelicals and charismatics' and he sets out to provide a corrective. 'Of all my books', he notes, 'this one has given me the most pain and the least pleasure to write.'[2] His subtitle is *Making Myths and Chasing Dreams*. He writes:

> It is tempting to suggest that Celtic Christianity is less an actual phenomenon defined in historical and geographical terms than an artificial construct created out of wishful thinking, romantic nostalgia, and the projection of all kinds of dreams about what should and might be.[3]

Dr Bradley quotes two earlier critiques of *Carmina Gadelica* in *Scottish Gaelic Studies* which are worth considering in some detail.

Hamish Robertson's attack

The first, a long paper published in 1976,[4] begins by commending Alexander Carmichael's 'zeal for the Gaelic' and his industry, and notes his contributions on Hebridean life, culture and economy in his evidence to the parliamentary Crofting Commission of 1884,[5] which were 'instrumental in bringing about a change of public opinion which had hitherto regarded the West Highlands and Isles as a cultural backwater whose sparse population spoke an uncouth language, and whose only contribution to the nation was seen to lie in candidates for soldiery and emigration'.[6] However, Hamish Robertson soon moves on to the attack.

He accuses Carmichael of 'literary exaggeration' and complains that he did not publish his footnotes in Gaelic[7] (which would hardly have helped to explain *Carmina Gadelica* to the outside world). He describes him as 'an artist [who] would touch up the expression of the Gael'; he alleges that Carmichael deliberately archaized his material, and that this indicated 'leanings towards duplicity';[8] and he repeatedly compares *Carmina Gadelica* to *Ossian*,[9] a well-known eighteenth-century forgery about a legendary third-century Irish warrior and bard, published in the early 1760s. *Ossian* was later discovered to be the invention of a Scottish poet, James Macpherson, and caused a notable scandal at the time.

Robertson goes on to claim that Carmichael wrote to advance a political cause, the plight of the crofters,[10] and that he 'resurrected Gaelic words of doubtful provenance'. Of the notes he had studied in Carmichael's 'rough hand', he says that 'words are substituted, many [poems] had alternative words at the end of the line, and even stacked up in threes and fours'. He alleges that Carmichael 'took it on himself to omit dubious material', and substantially altered the text. Verses had been switched round, lines lengthened or shortened, and he thought it possible that Carmichael had even invented lines or stanzas.[11]

Robertson had been through the Carmichael papers. In them he could find 'no trace of the [original] material existing for Vols. I and

II, except for a few rare passages which belong to the notes in the second volume'. He demands to know what has happened to the 'missing manuscripts' and even accuses some unnamed persons of having secretly hidden them.[12] He claims that Carmichael 'ascribed Gaelic lore to any but the Scottish Presbyterian tradition',[13] and had demonstrated 'an interest in Eastern religion' by 'making a journey in the imagination to India'.[14] Commenting on the story of the crofter who did not want his poem to be read by the cold eyes of foreigners, he comments that the destruction of the paper saved the crofter 'from the pious rigmarole of a romantic dilettante'.[15] On the editing of Volumes 3 and 4, he says that James Carmichael Watson showed 'an almost slavish respect . . . for the semi-sacred ideal of *Carmina Gadelica*, and a reluctance to offend Highland susceptibilities . . . not consonant with academic honesty'.[16]

Debates between academics in learned journals are not usually conducted in such a ferocious fashion. Who was Hamish Robertson, and what prompted this slashing attack? Ian Bradley does not mention the fact, but an editor's note preceding Robertson's paper in *Scottish Gaelic Studies* gives the information very clearly. He was a former postgraduate student in the Department of Celtic Studies in the University of Glasgow who 'did not complete his period of research' and was 'unlikely to return to it'.[17] These are the notes of a disappointed doctoral student – perhaps they amount to the sum total of his work on *Carmina Gadelica* before he abandoned it. The paper certainly expresses some frustrations – his dissatisfaction with Carmichael's transliteration of the Gaelic, his longing for a 'correct' text to which the rules of orthography could be applied, his notable lack of sympathy with Carmichael's religious tolerance in publishing poems with Catholic and 'pagan' origins, and his own inability to produce a doctoral thesis from such unpromising material.

It seems that Robertson was trying to treat *Carmina Gadelica* with the rigour which Calvinists applied to Holy Writ, and it was coming apart in his hands. Perhaps his supervisor should have noticed his problems before he reached the point of despair, and persuaded him to switch to a more manageable project. Robertson is described at the end of the paper as 'formerly of the University of Glasgow', and a literature search in the British Museum catalogue does not reveal any subsequent publications.

This angry outburst did not produce a reply from the University of Edinburgh, though one might have been expected. Alexander Carmichael lived in Edinburgh after he returned from the Isles, and had strong academic links with the University. His daughter Ella attended Professor Donald Mackinnon's Gaelic classes, Mackinnon wrote Carmichael's memoir in the *Celtic Review*, Mackinnon's successor was the Professor Watson who married Ella Carmichael, and their son was James Carmichael Watson, Professor of Celtic Studies in the same university.

The University of Glasgow seems to have played no part in the Carmichael saga until after World War Two, when Angus Matheson, of the Glasgow Department of Celtic Studies, edited Volume 5 from what was left of the Carmichael papers. Was it sheer accident that Hamish Robertson was a Glasgow student? Whatever the complexities of the relations between the two universities, or the two Departments of Celtic Studies, it seems probable that Edinburgh did not want to enter a major controversy. Instead, the reply was written, in very quiet and courteous terms, and perhaps with just a hint of unruffled *noblesse oblige*, from the laird of Canna.

John Lorne Campbell's response

John Lorne Campbell had corresponded with James Carmichael Watson while he was editing Volumes 3 and 4.[18] Campbell was a Gaelic-speaking antiquarian with a first-hand knowledge of the Isles. He is listed in the British Library catalogue as the author of 38 publications, mostly pamphlets and journal contributions, including a history of Canna, an edited book about life on Barra, and a biography of Father Allan McDonald of Eriskay, the Roman Catholic priest and folklorist who advised Alexander Carmichael.

Campbell describes the difficulties of working with Gaelic material, which was often to be found in several different fragmentary versions coming from different islands. 'How would *Carmina* have looked ... if different incomplete versions of the text had proliferated, with translations leaving gaps for unintelligible passages?'[19] The task of an editor was to 'tidy up' and select from his material in order to produce a publishable volume. Campbell notes – as Robertson does not – that a number of the poems were already known and published before *Carmina Gadelica* got into print, often in different versions originating on different islands. They were not all unknown, and some of them were very well known in Catholic circles. He regrets that neither Alexander Carmichael nor James Carmichael Watson was 'sufficiently acquainted with Catholic devotional literature to realise that some of the items they were publishing were Gaelic versions of well-known Catholic hymns'.[20]

John Lorne Campbell concludes that *Carmina Gadelica* was not 'an exercise in fabrication and deception' and that Robertson's paper contained substantial 'errors and misunderstandings'.[21] He thinks that Alexander Carmichael was a romantic, and that he could be 'irritatingly sentimental' at times; but he defends him and James Carmichael Watson very strongly against charges of dishonesty, at one point asking for a public apology and a retraction.[22]

Campbell judges James Carmichael Watson to have been 'a well-trained, conscientious and thorough scholar', which Alexander Carmichael of course was not; and he emphasizes Carmichael Watson's statement that he had used the existing translations, even when his own academic experience suggested a different rendering, because he did not have his grandfather's extensive knowledge of the oral traditions. Campbell thinks that Carmichael Watson was 'handicapped by an excessive *pietas* regarding his grandfather's work',[23] but makes it clear that he was dealing with very unsatisfactory material from an academic point of view, and doing his best with it. He insists that Carmichael and Carmichael Watson were both honourable men, and gives a very interesting account of how he thinks that Alexander Carmichael must have struggled with Gaelic orthography, trying to cope with 'numbers of strange words . . . uttered in various dialects'.[24] It cannot have been easy to catch what the Islanders were so softly crooning.

He concludes that *Carmina Gadelica* is an authentic study of the poetry of the Isles, though he too would like to see the original 'notebooks' – if they exist. He expresses a hope that someone would write a biography of Alexander Carmichael, with a full bibliography of both published and unpublished works.[25] To date, no one has taken on this task.

The Bradley version

In *Celtic Christianity*, Ian Bradley quotes and references both Hamish Robertson's paper and John Lorne Campbell's reply,[26] but without indicating to his readers their very different knowledge bases and religious affiliations. The Calvinist PhD student who had given up his studies in fury and the Roman Catholic antiquarian laird with a string of publications and a personal knowledge of how *Carmina Gadelica* was edited are treated without explanation as 'sources'; all Dr Bradley takes from either is criticism. From Robertson's paper, he repeats the charge that there are 'strong parallels' alleged between *Carmina Gadelica* and *Ossian*; that Carmichael deliberately archaized the language of the poems to make them seem older than they were, and endowed them with a 'spurious literary polish'; that he 'allowed his aversion to Calvinism . . . to distort their indigenous character by ascribing Gaelic sacred lore to all but the Scottish Presbyterian tradition'; and that he 'made a journey in the imagination to India' because of his 'interest in Eastern religion'. From John Lorne Campbell's paper he concludes that Campbell is 'kinder' to Carmichael than Robertson. Campbell 'refuses to see them [the poems] as an exercise in fabrication and deception', but he is quoted as deploring the absence of Carmichael's 'working notebooks', and thinking that he may well have tidied up and 'improved' poems. Bradley adds that this is done to emphasize the 'almost liturgical flavour' which makes them so popular for use in churches, but does not add Campbell's comment that many of them have liturgical origins. He makes no mention of Campbell's careful exposition of the working methods of Carmichael and Carmichael Watson.

Bradley's comments on the earlier critics contain substantial misunderstandings. It should be evident from Carmichael's Introduction and John Lorne Campbell's paper that *Carmina Gadelica* was not a forgery like *Ossian*. Alexander Carmichael spent 44 years tramping the Isles and collecting his material, and reproduced it to the best of his limited academic abilities. It was not subject to 'deliberate archaization'. The language into which he translated was the late Victorian Scottish-English of his own day, which is why a modern rendering may get closer to what the Islanders were singing in the first place. There is no sign of 'spurious literary polish': Carmichael was not a literary man, nor a polished writer, and he was so anxious to translate exactly what he heard and recorded, word for word, that the result often reads clumsily. The poems come from a religious environment centuries before the split between Catholic and Protestant, so it is hard to see how they can reflect an 'aversion to Calvinism'.

Bradley notes that Carmichael, in the preface to the first volume, says that some of the Songs 'may have been composed within the cloistered cells of Derry and Iona in the time of Columba and his followers'. This gentle speculation is dismissed.

> There were no cloisters in the monasteries of Iona or Derry in the time of Columba and his followers. Indeed there were no stone buildings of any kind. Iona got its first cloisters with the coming of the Benedictines in the twelfth century.[27]

This is a fairly basic misunderstanding. Benedictine cloisters were covered walkways adjacent to the church. They did not contain cells. Dictionary definitions of 'cloistered' refer not only to the Benedictine use, but to a more general meaning of 'cloistered' as monastic life or seclusion from the world. Alexander Carmichael was not referring to a particular style of architecture, but simply to quiet and remote places.

Bradley repeats Robertson's charge that Alexander Carmichael was able to gain the confidence of the Islanders who gave him his material because he was 'an exciseman checking up on illicit whisky production in the Highlands and Islands'.[28] Carmichael's work for the Inland Revenue Department concerned land taxation, not the illegal whisky trade.

Bradley's repetition of the statement that Carmichael 'made a journey in the imagination to India' and had an interest in Eastern religion may not worry ecumenical Christians, but it could alarm some strict Presbyterians. In fact, the charge rests on one brief passage in the Introduction to the first volume of *Carmina Gadelica*. Referring to an ancient tower at Rodail on Harris, which is carved with 'birds and beasts and reptiles and fishes, and of men and women, representing phallic worship', Carmichael writes:

Here pagan cult joins with Christian faith, the East with the West, the past with the present. The traveller from India to Scotland can here see, in the cold sterile rocks of Harris, the petrified symbols of a faith left living behind him on the hot, fertile plains of Hindustan. He can thus in his own person bridge over a space of eight thousand miles and a period of two thousand years.[29]

Perhaps it is the reference to phallic worship rather than to India that so offends the critics. It is difficult to comprehend why Carmichael mentioned India at all. Celtic Christianity was certainly affected by Eastern influences, but they were from the Middle East, from the Holy Land, from Syria and the Lebanon and the Thebaïd of Upper Egypt, not from the 'hot, fertile plains of Hindustan'. There is no suggestion that Carmichael ever visited India. Was he thinking of the gradual development of Indo-European languages through the centuries? Had he just attended a lecture (with pictures by magic lantern) by a missionary from India, and been reminded of Rodail?

John Lorne Campbell was right – he was a romantic; but whatever the story behind this brief passage, he could not have anticipated that this rather facile flight of fancy would be used to denigrate his beloved *Carmina* and his staunch Presbyterian beliefs.

Why has Dr Bradley resurrected this old controversy over *Carmina Gadelica*? To understand that, we have to turn to the context in which he wrote his book. The first indication comes from his foreword. He writes:

> The distinctive voice of the early indigenous Christians speaks to us through all the layers of distortion and fabrication with which it has been overlaid . . . this book is not about that voice or those people . . . only with how they came to be perceived in the centuries after their deaths.[30]

In other words, he is not writing about the original beliefs of Celtic Christians. He is writing about the later distortions of those beliefs. There are plenty of distortions to write about: the effect of the Danish invasions in the ninth century; Archbishop Lanfranc's ecclesiastical commission, which removed most of the indigenous saints from the Church calendars and substituted Continental ones after the Norman Conquest; the trade in relics, many of them false, in the time of the Crusades, and the unabashed commercialization of their new assets by the monasteries that followed; the extensive rewriting of the Lives of the Celtic saints undertaken in the twelfth and thirteenth centuries to make it appear that they had gone to Rome, submitted to the Pope, and probably been taught by St Germanus of Auxerre as well; the widespread destruction of monastic records and relics, some of them authentic, in Henry VIII's suppression of the monasteries; the even more drastic destruction of Scottish records in John Knox's time.

Dr Bradley does not appear to have a good grasp of this historical material, or of the many efforts that have been made by scholars to evaluate what material is still available. He dismisses it as 'a swamp of superstition'. He complains of 'the absence of hard facts' on Celtic Christianity,[31] but does not cite the many scholarly published sources available, many of them from the Irish University Press and the University of Wales Press, that list and evaluate early Celtic annals, chronicles and martyrologies.[32] Regrettably, no comparable work has been undertaken in Scotland since Bishop Alexander Forbes (Episcopalian bishop of Brechin) published his *Kalendars of Scottish Saints* in 1872.

The word 'saints' is a sticking point, because Dr Bradley assumes that it refers to the centralized processes of beatification and canonization instituted by the Roman Catholic Church; but as we have seen, the Celtic tradition uses 'saints' in the Pauline sense of the word. He seems to be arguing that it is not 'egalitarian' to regard some people as more holy than others, despite the fact that Calvinism, which he defends, involves a belief in predestination, which implies that some people are certainly holier than others, and there is nothing that the others can do about it.

Dr Bradley maintains that there is 'a misty and vague aura surrounding this age which accounts for its appeal'. This allows 'hagiographers, romantics and propagandists to weave myths and spin legends'. He is less than fair to modern hagiographers, who use the most up-to-date sources for their studies, and are constantly at work to expose the myths and legends on which popular imagination still feeds. Most of us do not now seriously believe that St Brigid hung her cloak on a sunbeam, or that an angel told Regulus to take the bones of St Andrew to the east coast of Fife in order to provide the Scots with a patron saint who would outrank the Irish Columba.

Since *Celtic Christianity* was published, Dr Bradley has produced *Colonies of Heaven: Celtic Models for Today's Church* (2000) in which he gives a more considered rationale for the earlier book. He explains that his first book, *The Celtic Way*, 'sold over twelve thousand copies' but 'with hindsight I can now see that it had rather too much of the over-romantic and uncritical enthusiasm of the new convert'. *Celtic Christianity* is, he explains, 'perhaps best seen as an act of penitence by someone who realised that his work had helped to fuel the current mood of Celto-mania' and who 'was conscious of the need for a critical academic study'.[33]

The book 'might seem to have taken me firmly into the camp of the academic sceptics and demythologisers', but he says that he has always maintained his belief in 'the Celtic voice'. He was only trying to clear away 'the layers of fabrication and distortion with which it has been overlaid'.[34]

Other writers on Celtic Christianity share this ambition, and also share Dr Bradley's dissatisfaction with the uncritical attitudes of the 'golden age' theorists, who find incredible legends 'charming' and continue to publish accounts of the Celtic saints that are all sweetness and light; but *Carmina Gadelica* is the raw material of academic study, not a flimsy exercise in wishful thinking.

A final context

Readers who have followed this convoluted story may ask why I have written this study. *Carmina Gadelica* has been composed, published and criticized in a number of sharply different contexts. So what is the present context? Why should a social historian based in York venture into this particular nest of Scots academic hornets? I am a Londoner by birth, Welsh by marriage, and with no Scots or Irish ancestry; a middle-of-the-road member of the Church of England, neither a Roman Catholic nor a Presbyterian. How did I get involved in the problems of *Carmina Gadelica*, the Collector, his grandson and the critics?

I have been working on aspects of Church history for some years – recently on Celtic saints, whose records have, as Dr Bradley says, often been distorted or badly mishandled over the centuries. Among the Celtic literature I found *Carmina Gadelica*, and I became fascinated by the ancient Celtic voices struggling to be heard through Alexander Carmichael's ponderous Victorian renderings. I am not a Gaelic speaker, but dictionaries and grammars helped. I discovered that many phrases that gave me particular delight, like the goats going up to the mountains of mist, or Christ lighting the stars, or the Man of the Night's exalted vision of the massed angels, were there in the Gaelic. Alexander Carmichael had not invented them or polished them or prettified them: the poetry was there already. I wanted to put the poems into plain English so that the devotional content could be appreciated by a wider readership, and the lives of the Islanders who crooned them more clearly understood; but I also came to form a considerable respect for Alexander Carmichael's work. With none of the advantages that   modern scholars take for granted – research grants, specialist study courses, trained assistants, office technology and the ability to scour the libraries of the world for information on the internet – he carried out his work by sheer dogged effort and personal commitment. He made a unique contribution to knowledge of the Isles, and one containing great spiritual resources for Christians well beyond the bounds of his native Scotland. His material is uneven, and we can only see the Islanders of a thousand years or more ago through a glass, darkly – but it is so much better than not seeing them at all.

The critics' accounts of how the poems were collected and edited contained hidden agendas and some fairly obvious biases. I thought it was time that all the different contexts were examined, and the Celtic voices were shaken free of the later voices that obscured them. It is as simple as that.

References

Part 1 The World of the Islanders

1 E. G. Bowen, *Saints, Seaways and Settlements in the Celtic Lands* (University of Wales Press, 1969, repr. 1977). See also Cyril Fox, *The Personality of Britain* (National Museum of Wales, 1943); T. O'Loughlin, 'Living in the Ocean', in Cormac Bourke (ed.), *Studies in the Cult of St Columba* (Four Courts Press, 1997), pp. 11–23; Simon Winchester, *The Map That Changed the World* (HarperCollins, 2001).

2 Barry Cunliffe, *Facing the Ocean: the Atlantic and its Peoples* (Oxford University Press, 2000).

3 Ninian: Bede, *Ecclesiastical History*, bk 3, ch. 25; 'Aelred's Life' in A. P. Forbes (ed.), *The Lives of St Ninian and St Kentigern* (1874); Peter Hill, *Whithorn and Ninian: Excavations of a Monastic Town* (Whithorn Trust, 1987) and *Whithorn: Excavations 1988–90* (Whithorn Trust, 1991).

4 Alistair Moffat, *The Sea Kingdoms* (HarperCollins, 2001), p. 55; Bowen, *Saints, Seaways and Settlements*, pp. 19–20.

5 Moffat, *op. cit.*, pp. 46–7. This account includes some interesting comments on modern curragh building and sailing.

6 Nora K. Chadwick, *The Celts*, (Penguin Books, 1970), p. 125.

7 Bowen, *Saints, Seaways and Settlements*, pp. 20–3, 35.

8 Richard Sharpe (trans. and ed.), *Adamnan's Life of Columba* (Penguin, 1995) p. 20.

9 Moffat, *op. cit.*, pp. 93, 106, follows the views of Julius Caesar and Pliny on the Druids, perhaps exaggerating their influence – and their cruelty. The Romans were always ready to believe the worst of barbarians.

10 Cunliffe, *Facing the Ocean*, Chs 1 and 2. The marvels and dangers thought to be present in the Ocean are expressed most vividly in the

account of the voyage of St Brendan the Navigator: see J. F. Webb, *Lives of the Saints* (Penguin Classics, 1965) for a translation – though this is an early romance rather than a historical account.

11 Myles Dillon and Nora Chadwick, *The Celtic Realms* (Weidenfeld & Nicholson, 1967), p. 174, quoting the *Chronicle* of Prosper Tiro, Bishop of Aquitaine. Also *Acta Sanctorum,* July, Vol. II, pp. 286–90.

12 Dillon and Chadwick, *op. cit.*, pp. 68–109.

13 *ibid.*

14 Michael Lynch, *Scotland: A New History* (Ebury Press, 1991), pp. 40–3.

15 Belisarius (503–65) was a Byzantine general.

16 For instance, Melania the Younger, a Roman heiress who, with her husband Pinian, successively abandoned their estates in central Italy, Sicily and north Africa under the threat of invasion, visited the Desert Fathers and ended her life in poverty as an anchorite. A Latin manuscript telling her story was found in the Escorial and published as *Santa Melania Giunore Senatrice Romana.* E. A. Clark, *The Life of Melania the Younger* (Edwin Mellen Press, 1984) gives an English version with a commentary.

17 See R. T. Meyer, *The Life and Letters of St Antony,* Ancient Christian Writers, Vol. 10, 1950; *Butler's Lives of the Saints,* ed. Paul Burns, 12 vols, Burns & Oates, 1998–2000, Jan., pp. 116–20.

18 P. Rousseau, *Pachomius* (University of California Press, 1985); D. J. Chitty, *The Desert a City* (Mowbray, 1977); *Butler's Lives of the Saints,* May, pp. 46–7.

19 J. N. D. Kelly, *Jerome: His Life, Writings and Controversies* (Duckworth, 1975) lists a number of ancient sources. See also H. F. D. Sparks, 'Jerome as Biblical Scholar' in *The Cambridge History of the Bible,* Vol. 1, (Cambridge University Press, 1970), pp. 510–41; *Butler's Lives of the Saints,* Sept., pp. 274–80.

20 See J. N. D. Kelly, *op. cit.*, for many references to Paula; F. Langrange, *Histoire de Sainte Paule* (1868); Kathleen Jones, *Women Saints* (Continuum, 1999), pp. 79–85.

21 D. Attwater, *The Golden Book of Eastern Saints* (Ayer Co. Pub., 1938), pp. 29–46; H. Bettenson, *The Later Christian Fathers* (Oxford University Press, 1972), pp. 59–98; *Butler's Lives of the Saints,* Jan., pp. 13–19, 64–6.

22 W. K. Lowther Clarke (trans. and ed.), *The Life of St Macrina* (1916); Jones, *Women Saints,* pp. 74–8.

23 E. R. Elder (ed.), *Benedictus: Studies in Honour of St Benedict of Nursia,*

(Continuum, 1981); Basil Hume, *In Praise of Benedict* (Hodder, 1981); D. H. Farmer (ed.), *Benedict's Disciples* (Gracewing, 1980); Esther de Waal, *Seeking God: The Way of St Benedict* (Fount, 1984).

24 L. Gougaud, *Christianity in Celtic Lands*, trans. Maud Joynt (1932); D. Pochin Mould, *The Irish Saints* (Burns & Oates, 1964); J. F. Kenney, *Sources for the Early History of Ireland: Ecclesiastical* (rev. L. Bieler, 1966); Richard Sharpe, *Medieval Irish Saints' Lives* (Clarendon Press, 1991); Kathleen Jones, *Who Are the Celtic Saints?* (Canterbury Press, 2002), Ch. 3, pp. 16–43.

25 Pelagius (*c.*360–420) was a Celtic monk, probably from Wales. His original name was Morgan, or 'sea-borne'. He was a wanderer who settled in Rome at the end of the fourth century, and wrote two treatises in which he denied the doctrine of original sin and predestination, maintaining that human beings had been created innocent, and possessed free will. The orthodox view in his time was that of his contemporary, St Augustine, who taught an extreme version of the doctrine of original sin. Pelagius was driven out of Rome and banished by Pope Zosimus.

26 L. Bieler (trans. and ed.), *The Irish Penitentials* (Dublin Institute for Advanced Studies, 1963).

27 Bede, *Ecclesiastical History*, bk 3, ch. 4; Nora K. Chadwick, *The Age of the Saints in the Early Celtic Church* (Oxford University Press, 1961), pp. 77–8.

28 D. Pochin Mould, *The Irish Saints*, pp. 169–71; *Butler's Lives of the Saints*, Sept., p. 171; J. F. Kenney, *Sources for the Early History of Ireland: Ecclesiastical*, p. 391.

29 Centralized procedures for the recognition of saints were instituted by Pope Innocent III (1199–1216) and regularized by Pope Urban VIII (1623–44).

30 L. Bieler (trans. and ed.), *The Works of St Patrick* (Irish Manuscripts Commission, 1952); A. B. A. Hood (trans. and ed.), *St Patrick: His Writings and Murchiu's Life* (Phillimore Press, 1978); R. C. P. Hanson, *The Life and Writings of the Historical St Patrick* (Seabury, 1983); E. A. Thompson, *Who Was St Patrick?* (1983).

31 *Acta Sanctorum*, Feb., vol. I, pp. 99–185 has Brigid's Latin Life by the monk Cogitosus; Lives in English include: A. Knowles, *Life of St Brigid* (Brown and Nolan, 1927); A. Curtayne, *St Brigid of Ireland* (Anthonian Press, 1931); F. O'Briain, *The Life of St Brigid* (1938); *Butler's Lives of the Saints*, Feb., pp. 1–5.

32 Bede, *Ecclesiastical History*, bk 3, chs 4 and 25, bk 5 ch. 9; Sharpe (trans. and ed.), *Adamnan's Life of Columba* pp. 10–11. Adamnan was the ninth abbot of Iona, and Columba's kinsman (Dillon and Chadwick, *Celtic Realms*, pp. 182–3).

33 Sharpe, *Adamnan's Life of Columba*, pp. 140, 184.

34 Sharpe, *op. cit.*, commentary, pp. 31–3.

35 Bede, *Ecclesiastical History*, bk 1, ch. 30.

36 See Murchiu's account in Hood (trans. and ed.), *St Patrick: His Life and Writings*. Murchiu was writing in the ninth century to advance the claims of the bishops of Armagh to be primates of Ireland. He complains about the accumulation of legends about St Patrick's ministry, and evidently this was one of them.

37 Dillon and Chadwick (*The Celtic Realms*, p. 108) give a slightly different terminology for these festivals; but since no writings have survived, the tradition is purely an oral one. The confident assertions of Sir James Frazer in *The Golden Bough* (1993 edn, pp. 517–22), on Druid ceremonies are now treated with considerable caution.

38 Dillon and Chadwick, *op. cit.*, pp. 13, 143–4.

39 A. Gwynn, *The Irish Monastery of Bangor*, Irish Ecclesiastical Records (Nov. 1950), pp. 385–97; *Butler's Lives of the Saints*, May, pp. 52–3.

40 Bede, *Ecclesiastical History*, bk 1, chs 23–34, bk 2, chs 9–17, 20, bk 3, chs 1–17, 25, 26; H. Mayr-Harting, *The Coming of Christianity to Anglo-Saxon England* (Batsford, 1972), pp. 102–16. The conflict is analysed in Kathleen Jones, *Who Are the Celtic Saints?*, pp. 203–41. Shirley Toulson, *The Celtic Alternative: A Reminder of the Christianity We Lost* (Century, 1985) mounts a passionate defence of the Celtic position at Whitby, but is often inaccurate.

41 Bede, *op. cit.*, bk 4, ch. 24.

42 Bede, *op. cit.*, bk 3, ch. 25.

43 Bede, *op. cit.*, bk 4, chs 27–32; Kenney, *op. cit.*, pp. 225–6; B. Colgrave, *Two Lives of St Cuthbert* (Cambridge University Press, 1940).

44 Edinburgh (Edwin's Burgh) was under the control of the king of Northumbria.

45 A. P. Forbes, *Kalendars of Scottish Saints* (1872), pp. 325–6; D. Pochin Mould, *Scotland of the Saints* (Batsford, 1952), pp. 142–9; *Butler's Lives of the Saints*, April, p. 117.

46 Moffat, *The Sea Kingdoms*, pp. 53–5, 286–7.

47 Moffat, *op. cit.*, p. 137. Dicuil was the author of a work entitled *World Geography*, and a monk at the Carolingian court.

48 R. Sharpe, introduction to *Adamnan's Life of Columba*, p. 83.
49 Moffat, *op. cit.*, p. 143.
50 Malcolm Canmore (1031–93) is the Malcolm best known as the prince who killed Macbeth in revenge for his father's murder.
51 Turgot's Life of St Margaret of Scotland is translated in J. Pinkerton, *Lives of the Scottish Saints* (1889), pp. 159–62; see also D. Baker (ed.), *Mediaeval Women* (Blackwell, 1979), pp. 119–41; Jones, *Women Saints*, pp. 121–7.
52 Moffat, *op. cit.*, p. 143.
53 Eusebius, *Historia Ecclesiastica* (Penguin Classics, 1959, repr. 1989), bk 3, chs 1, 25, 39; W. Skene, *Celtic Scotland* (1876), Vol. 1, pp. 296–9; Forbes, *Kalendars of Scottish Saints*, pp. 436–40.
54 Ian Bradley, *Celtic Christianity*, pp. 82–3.
55 See R. A. Mason (ed.), *John Knox and the British Reformations* (Ashgate, 1998); Lord Eustace Percy, *John Knox* (Hodder & Stoughton, 1937).

Part 2 Carmina Gadelica

Alexander Carmichael, *Carmina Gadelica: Hymns and Incantations* (Gaelic and English):
Vols 1 and 2, Norman Macleod, Edinburgh, 1912.
Vols 1 and 2, ed. E. C. C. Watson, reprinted, Oliver and Boyd, 1928.
Vol. 3, ed. James Carmichael Watson, Oliver and Boyd, 1940.
Vol. 4, ed. James Carmichael Watson, Oliver and Boyd, 1941.
Vol. 5, ed. Angus Matheson, Oliver and Boyd, 1952.

Selections from *Carmina Gadelica*:

G. R. D. MacLean (ed.), *Celtic Spiritual Verse: Poems of the Western Highlanders from the Celtic*, SPCK, 1961, repr. 2002.
Adam Bittlestone (ed.), *The Sun Dances: Prayers and Blessings from the Gaelic*, Floris Books, 1977.
Michael Jones (ed.), *New Moon of the Seasons*, Floris Books, 1986.
John MacInnes (ed.), *Carmina Gadelica: Hymns and Incantations Collected in the Highlands and Islands of Scotland in the Last Century by Alexander Carmichael*, Floris Books, 1992 (one volume with original drawings).

Part 3 Collecting and Editing *Carmina Gadelica*

1 Memoirs of Alexander Carmichael: Dr Kenneth Macleod, *Carmina Gadelica*, 1928 edn, Vol. 4, pp. xxi–v; Professor Donald Mackinnon, *Celtic Review*, iii, pp. 76–7.
2 Personal information from Mr Alistair Livingstone, Baron of Bachuill.
3 Mackinnon, *op. cit.*
4 Obituary in *The Times*, 10 June 1912, p. 9, col. b.
5 Alexander Carmichael, Introduction to Vol. 1 of *Carmina Gadelica*, 1928 edn, p. xxxiv.
6 Carmichael, *op. cit.*, p. xix.
7 *ibid.*
8 Mackinnon, *op. cit.*
9 Quoted by John Lorne Campbell, 'Notes on Hamish Robertson's Studies in Carmichael's *Carmina Gadelica*', *Scottish Gaelic Studies*, 1978, Vol. XIII, Part 1, p. 1.
10 *ibid.*
11 *Carmina Gadelica*, 1928 edn, p. xxxv.
12 *ibid.*
13 Campbell, *op. cit.*, p. 11.
14 Carmichael, *op. cit.*, p. xxxv.
15 *ibid.*
16 Mackinnon, *op. cit.*, p. 17.
17 Oliver and Boyd, Edinburgh, 1928.
18 Campbell, *op. cit.*, p. 4.
19 *op. cit.*, p. 5.
20 *Carmina Gadelica*, Vols 3 and 4, ed. James Carmichael Watson, 1940, 1941.
21 *Carmina Gadelica*, Vol. 5, ed. Angus Matheson, 1952.

Part 4 Critics and Contexts

1 Alexander Carmichael, Introduction to *Carmina Gadelica*, 1928 edn, Vol. 1, p. xxxix.
2 Ian Bradley, *Celtic Christianity* (Edinburgh University Press, 1999), p. vii.
3 *ibid.*
4 Hamish Robertson, 'Studies in Carmichael's *Carmina Gadelica*', *Scottish Gaelic Studies* XII (1976), Part 2, pp. 220–65.
5 Robertson, *op. cit.*, p. 224, quoting the Appendix to the Report of the

Crofting Commission, 1884, pp. 213–6 and 451–82.

6 Robertson, *op. cit.*, p. 224.

7 *op. cit.*, pp. 220–1.

8 *op. cit.*, p. 230.

9 *op. cit.*, pp. 224, 230, 240.

10 *op. cit.*, p. 224.

11 Numerous references: *inter al.*, *op. cit.*, pp. 225, 230, 231–2, 234, 238.

12 *op. cit.*, p. 226.

13 *op. cit.*, p. 240.

14 *op. cit.*, p. 240.

15 *op. cit.*, p. 236.

16 *op. cit.*, pp. 227–8.

17 *op. cit.*, p. 236.

18 John Lorne Campbell, 'Notes on Hamish Robertson's Studies in Carmichael's *Carmina Gadelica*', *Scottish Gaelic Studies*, XIII, 1978, Part 1, pp. 1–17. Canna is a small island in the same group as Rum, Muck and Eigg, to the south-west of Skye.

19 Campbell, *op. cit.*, p. 2.

20 *op. cit.*, p. 3.

21 *op. cit.*, p. 12.

22 *op. cit.*, p. 6.

23 *op. cit.*, p. 4.

24 *op. cit.*, p. 9.

25 *op. cit.*, p. 15.

26 Ian Bradley, *Celtic Christianity*, pp. 157–63.

27 Bradley, *op. cit.*, p. 159.

28 Bradley, *op. cit.*, p. 157.

29 Carmichael, *Carmina Gadelica*, 1928 edn, p. xxxix.

30 Bradley, *Celtic Christianity*, p. ix.

31 Bradley, *op. cit.*, p. 2.

32 For example, the *Liber Hymnorum*, Plummer's *Vitae Sanctorum Hiberniae*, Wade-Evans' *Vitae Sanctorum Britanniae et Genealogiae*, the ancient Scottish sources quoted by Bishop Forbes in his *Kalendars of Scottish Saints*, or such modern works as *Butler's Lives of the Saints* or Lapidge and Sharpe's *Bibliography of Celtic-Latin Literature, 400–1200* (Royal Irish Academy, 1985).

33 Ian Bradley, *Colonies of Heaven* (Darton, Longman and Todd, 2000), pp. vii–viii.

34 Bradley, *Colonies of Heaven*, pp. viii–ix.

Bíblíography

Acta Sanctorum, 64 vols, Antwerp, 1643– . Also published in Rome and Paris.

Adam, David, *The Edge of Glory: Prayers in the Celtic Tradition*, SPCK, 1985.

Annals of Tigernach, ed. Whitley Stokes, *Revue Celtique*, 16 (1895), 17 (1896), 18 (1897).

Annals of Ulster, S. MacAirt and G. MacNiocaill (eds), Part 1, Text and Translation to AD 1131, Dublin Institute for Advanced Studies, 1983.

Armagh: The Book of Armagh, ed. J. Gwynn, Dublin, 1913.

Attwater, Donald, *The Golden Book of Eastern Saints*, Ayer Co. Pub., 1938.

Baker, D. (ed.), *Mediaeval Women*, Blackwell, 1979.

Bede, *Ecclesiastical History of the English People* and *Letter to Egbert*, trans. Leo Shirley-Price, Penguin Classics, 1955, revised edn 1990.

Bettenson, H. (ed.), *The Later Christian Fathers*, Oxford University Press, 1972.

Bieler, L. (trans. and ed.), *The Works of St Patrick*, Irish Manuscripts Commission, 1953.

Bieler, L. (ed.), *The Irish Penitentials*, Dublin Institute for Advanced Studies, 1963.

Bittleston, Adam (ed.), *The Sun Dances: Prayers and Blessings from the Gaelic*, Floris Books, 1977.

Bowen, E. G., *Saints, Seaways and Settlements in the Celtic Lands*, University of Wales Press, 1969, repr. 1977.

Bradley, Ian, *The Celtic Way*, Darton, Longman and Todd, 1993, repr. 2000.

Bradley, Ian, *Columba, Pilgrim and Penitent*, Wild Goose Publications, 1996.

Bradley, Ian, *Celtic Christianity: Making Myths and Chasing Dreams*, Edinburgh University Press, 1999, repr. 2001.

Bradley, Ian, *Colonies of Heaven: Celtic Models for Today's Church*, Darton, Longman and Todd, 2000.

Butler's Lives of the Saints, ed. Paul Burns, 12 vols, Burns & Oates, 1998–2000.

Campbell, John Lorne, 'Notes on Hamish Robertson's Studies in *Carmina Gadelica*', *Scottish Gaelic Studies*, XIII, 1978, Part 2, pp. 1–27.

Carmichael, Alexander (ed.), *Carmina Gadelica: Hymns and Incantations*, (Gaelic and English), Vols 1 and 2, Edinburgh, 1912; Vols 1 and 2, ed. E. C. C. Watson, reprinted, Edinburgh, 1928; Vols 3 and 4, ed. James Carmichael Watson, 1940 and 1941 respectively; Vol. 5, ed. Angus Matheson, 1952.

Chadwick, Nora K., *The Age of the Saints in the Early Celtic Church*, Oxford University Press, 1961.

Chadwick, Nora K., *The Celts*, Pelican Books, 1970.

Chitty, D., *The Desert City: An Introduction to the Study of Egyptian and Palestinian Monasticism under the Christian Empire*, Mowbray, 1977.

Clark, E. A. (ed.), *The Life of Melania the Younger*, Edwin Mellen Press, 1984.

Colgrave, B., *Two Lives of St Cuthbert*, Cambridge University Press, 1940.

Cunliffe, Barry, *Facing the Ocean: The Atlantic and its Peoples 8000 BC to AD 1500*, Oxford University Press, 2001.

Curtayne, A. *St Brigid of Ireland*, Anthonian Press, 1931.

de Waal, Esther, *Seeking God: The Way of St Benedict*, Fount, 1984.

de Waal, Esther, *The Celtic Vision*, Liguori Publications, 1988, repr. 1991.

de Waal, Esther, *A World Made Whole*, Fount, 1991.

de Waal, Esther, *The Celtic Way of Prayer*, Hodder & Stoughton, 1996, repr. 2003.

Dillon, Myles, and Nora Chadwick, *The Celtic Realms*, Weidenfeld & Nicholson, 1967, repr. 2000.

Elder, E. R. (ed.), *Benedictus: Studies in Honour of St Benedict*, Continuum, 1981.

Eusebius, *The History of the Church (Historia Ecclesiastica)*, Penguin Classics, 1959, repr. 1989.

Farmer, D. H. (ed.), *Benedict's Disciples*, Gracewing, 1980.
Félire: Whitley Stokes (ed.), *The Martyrology of Oengus the Culdee*, 1905.
Forbes, A. P., *Kalendars of Scottish Saints*, Edinburgh, 1872.
Forbes, A. P., *The Lives of St Ninian and St Kentigern*, Edinburgh, 1874.
Fox, Cyril, *The Personality of Britain: Its influence on inhabitant and invader in prehistoric and early historic times*, National Museum of Wales, 1943.
Frazer, Sir James, *The Golden Bough*, 1922, Wordsworth Editions, 1993.

Gougaud, L., *Christianity in Celtic Lands*, trans. Maud Joynt, Sheed and Ward, 1932.
Gwynn, A., *The Irish Monastery of Bangor*, Irish Ecclesiastical Records, Nov. 1950.

Hanson, R. C. P., *The Life and Writings of the Historical St Patrick*, Seabury, 1983.
Hill, Peter, *Whithorn and Ninian: Excavations of a Monastic Town*, Whithorn Trust, 1987.
Hill, Peter, *Whithorn: Excavations 1988–90*, Whithorn Trust, 2001.
Hood, A. B. A., *St Patrick: His Writings and Murchiu's Life*, Phillimore Press, 1978.
Hume, Basil (Cardinal), *In Praise of Benedict*, Hodder, 1981.

Jones, Kathleen, *Women Saints*, Continuum, 1999.
Jones, Kathleen, *Who Are the Celtic Saints?*, Canterbury Press, 2002.
Jones, Michael (ed.), *New Moon of the Seasons: Prayers from the Highlands and Islands*, Floris Books, 1986.

Kelly, J. N. D., *Jerome: His Life, Writings and Controversies*, Duckworth, 1975.
Kenney, J. F., *Sources for the Early History of Ireland: Ecclesiastical*, New York, 1929, revised by L. Bieler, Dublin, 1966.
Knowles, A., *Life of St Brigid*, Brown and Nolan, 1927.

Langrange, R., *Histoire de Sainte Paule* (1868).
Lapidge, Michael and Richard Sharpe, *A Bibliography of Celtic-Latin Literature, 400–1200*, Royal Irish Academy, 1985.
Leechdoms, Wortcunning and Starcraft of Early England, O. Cockayne (ed.), 3 vols, Rolls Series, HMSO, item 35, 1864–66.
Liber Hymnorum: J. H. Bernard and R. Atkinson (eds), *The Irish Liber Hymnorum*, 2 vols, Henry Bradshaw Society, 1898.

songs of the isles

Lowther Clarke, W. H. (trans and ed.), *The Life of St Macrina*, SPCK, 1916.

Lynch, Michael, *Scotland: A New History*, Ebury Press, 1991.

MacInnes, John (ed.), *Carmina Gadelica: Hymns and Incantations Collected in the Highlands and Islands of Scotland in the Last Century by Alexander Carmichael*, Floris Books, 1992.

MacLean, G. R. D. (ed.), *Celtic Spiritual Verse: Poems of the Western Highlanders from the Celtic*, SPCK, 1961, repr. 2002.

Mason, R. A. (ed.), *John Knox and the British Reformations*, Ashgate, 1999.

Matheson, Angus (ed.), *Carmina Gadelica*, Vol. 5, Edinburgh, 1952.

Mayr-Harting, H., *The Coming of Christianity to Anglo-Saxon England*, Batsford, 1972.

Meyer, R. T. (ed.), *The Life and Letters of St Antony*, Ancient Christian Writers, Vol. 10, Newman Press, 1950.

Moffat, Alistair, *The Sea Kingdoms: The History of Celtic Britain and Ireland*, HarperCollins, 2001.

O'Briain, F., *The Life of St Brigid*, 1938.

O'Loughlin, T., 'Living in the Ocean', in *Studies in the Cult of St Columba*, ed. Cormac Bourke, Four Courts Press, 1997, pp. 11–23.

Percy, (Lord) Eustace, *John Knox*, Hodder & Stoughton, 1937.

Pinkerton, J., *Ancient Lives of the Scottish Saints*, Alexander Gardner, 1889.

Plummer, Charles, *Vitae Sanctorum Hiberniae* (Vol. 1, in Irish), *The Lives of the Irish Saints* (Vol. 2, in English), Oxford University Press, 1910, repr. 1968.

Pochin Mould, Daphne, *Scotland of the Saints*, Batsford, 1952.

Pochin Mould, Daphne, *The Irish Saints*, Burns & Oates, 1964.

Robertson, Hamish, 'Studies in *Carmina Gadelica*', Scottish Gaelic Studies XII, 1976, Part 2, pp. 221–65.

Rousseau, P., *Pachomius: The Making of a Community in Fourth Century Egypt*, University of California Press, 1985.

Sharpe, Richard, *Medieval Irish Saints' Lives: An introduction to Vitae Sanctorum Hiberniae*, Clarendon Press, 1991.

Sharpe, Richard (trans. and ed.), *Adamnan of Iona: Life of Columba*, Penguin, 1995.

Sheldrake, P., *Living Between Worlds: Place and Journey in Celtic Spirituality*, Darton, Longman and Todd, 1995.

Skene, W., *Celtic Scotland*, 3 vols, 1876.

Sparks, H. F. D., 'Jerome as Biblical Scholar', *Cambridge History of the Bible*, Vol. 1, Cambridge University Press, pp. 510–41.

Thompson, E. A., *Who Was St Patrick?*, 1983.

Toulson, Shirley, *The Celtic Alternative: A Reminder of the Christianity We Lost*, Century, 1985.

van de Weyer, R., *Celtic Fire*, Darton, Longman and Todd, 1990, repr. 1997.

Wade-Evans, A. W., *Vitae Sanctorum Britanniae et Geneologiae*, Cardiff, 1944.

Watson, James Carmichael (ed.), *Carmina Gadelica*, Vol. 3, Edinburgh 1940, Vol. 4, Edinburgh 1941.

Webb, J. F., *Lives of the Saints*, Penguin Classics, 1965.

Winchester, Simon, *The Map That Changed the World: The Tale of William Smith and the Birth of a Science*, HarperCollins, 1971.

An Invitation to JOIN THE FRIENDS OF

SCM-CANTERBURY PRESS

And save money on your religious book buying ...

Friends of SCM-Canterbury Press is a superb value-for-money membership scheme offering massive savings on both imprints.

BENEFITS OF MEMBERSHIP

- *Exclusive: 20% off all new books published in the year*
- *Exclusive: offers at 50% or more off selected titles from the backlist*
- *Exclusive: offers on Epworth Press and other distributed lists*
- *Exclusive: dedicated website pages, e-mail bulletins, special offers and competitions*

Join now – and start saving money on your book-buying today!

If you would like to join please contact:
The Mailing List Secretary, SCM-Canterbury Press,
9-17 St Albans Place, London N1 0NX
Tel: 00 44(0) 207 359 8034 • Fax: 00 44 (0) 207 359 0049
Email: office@scm-canterburypress.co.uk
PLEASE QUOTE BOOKAD

Alternatively why not join online and gain an extra saving of £1; the members' pages are very easy to use and all online ordering is completely secure.

Join at: www.scm-canterburypress.co.uk/members
Subscriptions run annually.
2004 Rates: UK £7.00 • International: £9.00